Ta

MW00761092

Welcome to the Junior Electives Series

 Let's talk about it . . .

What is it like to grow up in America today? How do our Junior-age children perceive the world around them, and their place in it? Did you know that your Junior students are more aware of the world around them than any previous generation of American children? However, seen through their eyes the world is often seen as a scary and anxious place. Every day they are blatantly confronted with the threat of nuclear disasters, ecological concerns that warn them their planet may not exist by the time they grow up, and an increasing number of their classmates either wielding knives and guns at school or killed in gang-related incidents. Closer to home, you can expect a high number of your students to have experienced at least one divorce in their family, or suffered some kind of physical, sexual, or emotional abuse from family members.

As adults, we may like to close our eyes and see the days of childhood as carefree and innocent as they might have been in our day. But when we open our eyes and see the world as our kids see it today, it is clear that life holds much stress and anxiety for our children. Instead of wishing for simpler days, it is time for us to say to our kids, "Let's talk about it . . ."

The Junior Electives Series was designed to help you do just that. Each topic in the series was selected because it represents issues Juniors are concerned about, and in many cases learning about from their peers, the media, or in school. With the help of this curriculum, you will be able to provide an opportunity for them to discuss their concerns in a Christian context. For many of your kids, this may be the first chance they will have to hear that the Bible has a lot to teach them about each of these contemporary life concerns.

As you teach the lessons in this series, you will have an opportunity to:
• Introduce and teach topics of concern to Juniors in a distinctively Christian context.
• Provide a safe place to learn about, talk about, and express feelings about each issue.

• Teach practical skills and biblical principles Juniors can use to cope with each concern in their daily lives.
• Provide a tool to help parents facilitate family discussion and coping in the home setting.

 Features of the Junior Elective Series

Four-Part Lesson Plan

Each lesson follows this format:

1. Setting the Stage (5-10 minutes). Each lesson begins with an activity designed to do two things. First, it is a gathering activity, meaning that you can involve your students in it as soon as they arrive. You do *not* need to have the whole class present to begin your lesson time. By arriving early and having the Setting the Stage activity set up and ready for the kids as soon as they walk in the door, you will communicate a sense of excitement about the lesson and set a tone of orderliness for your class.

Second, the Setting the Stage activity is purposeful in that it will draw the students into the subject for the day. It is more than just something to keep the kids busy while everyone arrives. The activity will provide a fun and interesting way to draw the kids' attention to an area of interest in their lives. Most of the time, it will also raise questions which will lead them into the next section of the lesson.

2. Introducing the Issue (20 minutes). Building on the Setting the Stage activity, this section of the lesson will involve the kids in an active discussion of the topic of the day. The material provided for you contains information the kids need to know, anticipating key questions they may have. It also includes one or more learning activities particularly designed to encourage your students to talk about the issues most on their minds, while in the context of a Christian community. To make this time as effective as possible, you will need to establish your class as a safe place where everyone's feelings and questions are welcomed and treated seriously (some suggestions for doing that are listed on page 5). Once that has been accomplished, you may be surprised at how much your Juniors have to say, and the depth of their thinking!

3. Searching the Scriptures (20 minutes). This section of each lesson takes your class to the Bible to discover what God has to say about the topic being discussed. Your students may be amazed to find out just how much the Bible says about subjects that seem

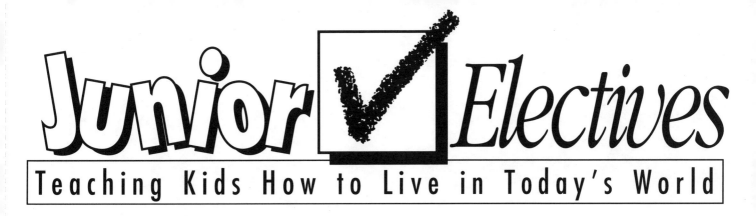

Junior ✓ Electives
Teaching Kids How to Live in Today's World

Peer Pressure
Pain & Death
Heroes

Linda Kondracki,
Bev Gundersen and Debbie Rempfer

David C. Cook Publishing Co.
Elgin, Illinois/Weston, Ontario

David C. Cook Publishing Co.
Elgin, Illinois/Weston, Ontario
Junior Elective Series: Peer Pressure, Pain & Death, Heroes
©1992 David C. Cook Publishing Co.

Published by David C. Cook Publishing Co.
850 N. Grove Avenue, Elgin, IL 60120
Cable Address: DCCOOK
Series Editor: Ellen Larson
Designed by Jeff Jansen
Illustrated by Sonny Carder
Printed in U.S.A.

ISBN: 1-55513-751-2

so *modern*. Through a wide variety of creative teaching methods, your class will study people and principles of Scripture that speak directly to the concerns gripping their hearts and minds. As you study together, you will also be acquainting them with the most valuable resource they can have for coping with these contemporary issues: their Bibles.

4. Living the Lesson (5-10 minutes). The final section of each lesson challenges the kids to take what they've learned and apply it to their own lives. It's the *so what* section. The class members will be encouraged to ask themselves, "So what am I going to do with what I've just learned?"

Clearly Stated Key Principles

Each book in the Junior Electives Series contains three units, each of which addresses a different topic of concern. The following three unit features will help your students focus on and remember the central principles of each unit.

1. Unit Verse. One verse has been chosen for each unit that summarizes the biblical principle central to the unit topic. The meaning of this verse is developed a little more each week as students work on a cooperative learning activity designed to help them understand and apply a key biblical principle.

2. Unit Affirmation. The primary learning objective for each unit has been phrased into an affirmation sentence that begins with "I can . . ." Discussing this affirmation each week will empower your students by letting them know they can do something positive about issues that may feel frightening or overwhelming.

3. Unit Service Projects. At the end of each unit you will find several ideas for your class not only to learn about the unit issue, but actually DO something about it. Although they are optional, taking the extra time to involve your class in a unit project will help them practice new skills and see for themselves that they can take an active role in the issues that affect their lives.

Parent Informational Letter

At the beginning of each unit, you will find PART-NERS . . . , a newsletter that you can photocopy and send home to the parents of your class members. This letter gives parents an overview of the topic being studied, as well as some practical ideas of ways they can further their child's learning through several Do-At-Home activities.

Flexibility and Variety

The Junior Electives Series has been designed to be usable in any number of settings. It is equally effective in a Sunday-school setting, a Wednesday-night series, or even a special setting such as a weekend retreat. If you live in an area that participates in release time, this series is an exellent resource to present biblical principles in a contemporary way. Feel free to be creative and find the best place for your group to talk about these important life principles.

A variety of learning activities are used to present the issue information and biblical truths. The following materials are considered standard supplies and are recommended to be available for the classtimes:

- Bibles   • Glue   • Tape
- Pencils   • Scissors   • Stapler
- Paper

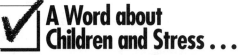

A Word about Children and Stress . . .

As you prepare to teach the Junior Electives Series, it is important to realize that many of the subjects you will be studying are the sources of stress in the lives of your students. Many students may never have had the chance to talk openly about these issues, and doing so in your class may well raise their anxiety level. Throughout these sessions, there are several things you can keep in mind:

1) Point them to Jesus. Perhaps the greatest benefit of the Junior Elective Series is that it will give you the opportunity to help your kids learn that a relationship to Jesus Christ is the best resource we can have to face the stressful, anxious parts of our lives. Through the Bible studies and your own personal witness of the power of Christ in your life, you can have the privilege of introducing children to Jesus and inviting them to ask Him to be an active part of their lives.

2) Create a safe place where they can talk about their real feelings. Children have a strong tendency to say the things in class that they think teachers want to hear. Early on in this series, you will want to create a safe place for sharing by continually reassuring your kids that they can say what is really on their minds, and making a rule that no one can criticize or make fun of anything anyone else shares in class. In many cases, expressing their feelings in a safe place, and having those feelings accepted by you and the class will relieve much of their anxiety.

3) If necessary, help them get outside help. You may find a child in your class who is experiencing an unusual amount of stress. In that case, ask your pastor or Christian Education Director for the procedure your church uses to refer children and families for professional help.

Who Do We Follow? . . .

From the beginning of time, God created people to live and function in groups. However, groups can often mean pressures and pressures can be difficult for people of any age to recognize and handle. In a society where there seems to be decreasing time for Juniors to interact with their families, peers are a major source of personal identity. Junior-age kids may follow the crowd without even thinking through who or what they're following, or what the consequences might be. But when they're given a little encouragement by someone else (a teacher, parent, and especially a peer) and made aware of their potential, the entire decision–making process and friendship abilities can flourish.

In this unit, you'll have the opportunity to help your Juniors discover that the mysterious stress and pressures they think they are feeling really do exist. It's called peer pressure. These pressures are something they can learn to control, and the mysteries of their influences can be uncovered. The students will be learning things like how to recognize pressures, whether the pressures are good or bad, and ways to reverse the negative pressures. Through games, Scripture, cartoon characters, and more you'll be able to help your kids learn that they can think for themselves, can be (and have) genuine friends, and can also help influence others to follow God's ways.

Peer Pressure Overview

Unit Verse: Do not conform any longer to the pattern of this world, but be transformed by the renewing of your mind. Romans 12:2

Unit Affirmation: I CAN LEARN TO THINK FOR MYSELF!

LESSON	TITLE	OBJECTIVE	SCRIPTURE BASE
Lesson #1	Carbon-Copy Conformity	That your students will recognize ways others place pressure on them to think and act like they do.	I Kings 22:1-28
Lesson #2	The Choice Is Yours	That your students will learn to make wise decisions by considering potential results instead of what others say.	Judges 16:4-22
Lesson #3	A Different Approach	That your students will learn techniques they can use to reverse negative peer pressure and still keep their friends.	I Samuel 24:1-22
Lesson #4	United We Stand	That your students will discover methods to help them maintain positive decision-making skills.	Numbers 13:16-19, 26-30; 14:22-24; Joshua 1:1-9
Lesson #5	That's What Friends Are For	That your students will understand that real friends care about each other and use positive methods to influence others to follow God's ways.	Daniel 1:8-20

Partners

For the next few weeks your Junior-age child will be part of a group learning about Peer Pressure. *Partners* is a planned parent piece to keep you informed of what will be taught during this exciting series.

PREVIEW...

Peer Pressure

Today, Junior-age kids face a variety of pressures. With the availability of drugs and pornography, news reports on teen suicides, the general amorality of society, and a growing awareness of the occult, our kids are confronted with difficult decisions earlier than ever before—and often by close friends. But it isn't all negative. Kids have the hope found in God's enabling them to make wise decisions, in His empowering them to handle peer pressure, and through the examples He's provided for us

in the Bible. God gives us as parents and teachers the peace and wisdom we need to help kids deal with peer pressure and learn to think through the consequences of conformity or nonconformity.

In the next few weeks, your child will have the opportunity to explore and talk about peer pressure. This unit is designed to encourage each child to think through a situation and learn to make wise decisions. The class will begin to recognize ways others use pressure and discover how negative peer pressure can be reversed, influencing others to follow God's ways.

Unit Verse:

Do not conform any longer to the pattern of this world, but be transformed by the renewing of your mind. Romans 12:2

Unit Affirmation:

I CAN LEARN TO THINK FOR MYSELF!

PRINCIPLES...

Peer Pressure

PRINCIPLE #1:
OTHERS PLACE PRESSURE ON US TO THINK AND ACT LIKE THEY DO.

Learning to recognize peer pressure is an important step toward maturity. This pressure to do what someone else wants us to do can be so subtle that we may not even be aware of it.

PRINCIPLE #2:
CONSIDER POTENTIAL RESULTS INSTEAD OF WHAT OTHERS SAY.

Peer pressure can influence us to listen to what others say instead of "thinking it through" for ourselves. We learn to make

wise decisions when we first consider the choices and possible consequences of an action.

PRINCIPLE #3:
NEGATIVE PEER PRESSURE CAN BE REVERSED.

Peer pressure is influential in a variety of ways. It doesn't have to be something to avoid; we can learn to use our own influence to turn the pressure away and still keep our friends.

PRINCIPLE #4:
MAINTAIN POSITIVE DECISION-MAKING SKILLS.

The positive effects of peer pressure are encouraged when we examine the biblical responsibility to help each other and work together.

PRINCIPLE #5:
REAL FRIENDS CARE ABOUT EACH OTHER AND HELP OTHERS FOLLOW GOD'S WAYS.

True friendship involves caring enough to be there to help and provide support. Learning how to be a friend and provide this help is an ongoing process. The responsi-

bilities that come with friendship also means using positive methods to influence others to follow Christ.

PRACTICE...

Peer Pressure
1. POST YOUR FAMILY GUIDELINES.

Base your family guidelines on the Word of God; the strength of our standards comes from their Originator. Write out your family guidelines and post them for all to see. These guidelines could include such things as television, friendships, attitudes, vocabulary, activities, music, and possessions and apply to all family members as well as baby-sitters and friends staying over.

2. LISTEN ACTIVELY AND TOGETHER.

Watch television and listen to music together. Take advantage of the remote's mute button during commercials and the *dead* time between songs to talk about the pressures you see and hear. Encouraging

active TV viewing and music listening helps to teach discretion and reinforces *thinking it through.* Maintain the same guideline for yourself as you expect for your child: "If you wouldn't do it or say it, don't watch it or sing it."

3. BE PRESENT IN YOUR CHILD'S LIFE.

Take the opportunity to be involved in your Junior's life through band boosters, scouting leadership, sports coaching, and teaching. You can also be present by being a snack provider, a group car driver, and by being home when your child has friends over. Take the initiative to become well acquainted with your child's friends.

4. SHARE BIBLE STUDY AND PRAYER.

Help your child develop daily Bible study and prayer time, both personally and as a family. Use this as a time to talk about contemporary heroes to admire and the desirable qualities of our models as described in the Bible.

Carbon-Copy Conformity

Aim: That your students will recognize ways others place pressure on them to think and act like they do.

Scripture: I Kings 22:1-28

Unit Verse: Do not conform any longer to the pattern of this world, but be transformed by the renewing of your mind.
Romans 12:2

Unit Affirmation: I CAN LEARN TO THINK FOR MYSELF!

 **Planning Ahead**

1. Photocopy Activity Sheets (page 15 and 16)—one for each student.
2. Write leader cards for Simon Says as described in SETTING THE STAGE.
3. Prepare the Unit Affirmation poster by writing the following title across the top of a large poster board. I CAN LEARN TO THINK FOR MYSELF! Under the title, write the numbers 1-5 vertically down the left-hand side.
4. Prepare the materials for the Unit Verse Activity by writing the Unit Verse on a piece of paper 12" x 36" and attaching it to the wall. Have a 36" wide roll of butcher paper (available at school supply stores) and about 4' - 5' of paper for each student to make a life-size Unit Verse Pattern.
5. Use small pieces of paper to write the following instructions. Write each instruction on enough papers to give to half the students. 1. **LOOK:** WITHOUT SAYING ANYTHING, BEGIN LOOKING AT THE CEILING AND KEEP LOOKING UNTIL I SAY STOP. 2. **LAUGH:** WITHOUT SAYING ANYTHING, BEGIN LAUGHING AND KEEP LAUGHING UNTIL I SAY STOP.

1 Setting the Stage (5-10 minutes)

WHAT YOU'LL DO

- Play Simon Says to illustrate conforming to the group

WHAT YOU'LL NEED

- Leader cards

2 Introducing the Issue (20 minutes)

WHAT YOU'LL DO

- Discuss ways others influence us and the power of peer pressure
- Use an activity sheet to identify ways influence is used
- Begin the Unit Affirmation poster

WHAT YOU'LL NEED

- "Pressure Characters" Activity Sheet (page 15)
- Unit Affirmation poster

3 Searching the Scriptures (20 minutes)

WHAT YOU'LL DO

- Roleplay one man's experience of standing against peer pressure
- Make life-size Unit Verse Patterns

WHAT YOU'LL NEED

- **OPTIONAL:** costumes and props appropriate to the Bible story
- Butcher paper

4 Living the Lesson (5-10 minutes)

WHAT YOU'LL DO

- Use an activity sheet to practice identifying peer pressure

WHAT YOU'LL NEED

- "Hidden Pressures" Activity Sheet (page 16)
- Balloons—two for each student

Lesson 1

 ## Setting the Stage (5-10 minutes)

Before class, write instructions on separate pieces of paper for each student, and add a different way to lead on each piece. For example: WHEN YOU ARE THE LEADER, TRY TO CONFUSE THE PLAYERS. HERE IS ONE SUGGESTION: "Simon says, scratch the ear of the person next to you." or WHEN YOU ARE THE LEADER, TRY TO CONFUSE THE PLAYERS. HERE IS ONE SUGGESTION: "Simon says, lift your right foot while touching your left elbow to your right knee." or WHEN YOU ARE THE LEADER, TRY TO CONFUSE THE PLAYERS. HERE IS ONE SUGGESTION: "Scratch your nose (but you scratch your chin)."

As the students arrive, give each one a piece of paper with the instructions. Set up a clock with an alarm or appoint a timekeeper to change leaders every 60-90 seconds. Begin to play Simon Says with the first students. As more kids come, ask each leader to use more challenging, complicated, and faster commands. At the conclusion of the game, talk about the pressure of doing what the leader demanded.

We just played a game where we all tried to be alike and had to follow the instructions of the leader. In many areas of our lives, when it is not a game, others put pressure on us to think and act like they do. Sometimes the pressures are easy to see, but other times the messages may be subtle, they're not something we're aware of. **Today we're beginning a new unit about peer pressure and decision making—somethings that can be hard to deal with. But God has provided examples for us of how to handle pressure. He wants to help us use His guidelines to think for ourselves. In the next few weeks we'll talk and learn about God's plan for peer pressure.**

 ## Introducing the Issue (20 minutes)

What is peer pressure? Discuss the students' understanding of these words and the assumptions they have about the words, then present a clear definition. **A peer is anyone about your same age with similar interests and abilities. Pressure is someone trying to get you to do something because that other person wants you to do it. Who are your peers?** (Kids in every part of your life, including television, commercials, and books.)

Give half the students a piece of paper with the LOOK instructions on it as described in Planning Ahead. Tell the other half of the class that they will have some instructions in a few minutes. As the first half of the class begins to look at the ceiling, call attention to the behavior of the rest of the class. **Why were**

you looking at the ceiling? (Everyone was doing it.) Give the second half of the class the LAUGH instruction slips. As they begin to laugh, notice the behavior of those without the written instructions. **Why are you laughing?** (Because the others are.)

Do you feel influenced by your peers? In what ways? Talk about whether other kids try to make you be like themselves or whether you just want to be like those you see and hear. Use a wide range of subjects in this discussion, such as clothes, music, food, school supplies, toys, and sports interests. **Do you think it is good or bad to be like your peers?**

When can peer pressure be good, be positive? What are some good influences you see and hear? Use a chalkboard or poster board to list the students' responses, with positive responses on the left side and negative on the right side. Possibilities of positive peer pressure are: group of friends study together for a test, cheering each other on to finish the relay in gym, the coach making the team exercise and practice each day, working or saving toward a goal. **What are some negative pressures?** (Asking for help to cheat on a test, copying homework, lying, betting on a football game, shoplifting, smoking, making fun of those who don't conform, "just-one-time-won't-hurt" reasoning, gossiping, foul language, drugs and alcohol use.) **When people use pressure on you, their goal is to have you do what *they* want to do and this gives them power over you.**

There are some key characters that can illustrate the kinds of pressure some people use on others. Be on the lookout for The Victim, The Salesman, The Enemy Agent, The Brat, The Sympathy Seeker, and The Bully! Distribute copies of the activity sheet "Pressure Characters" (page 15). Give students a chance to look over the illustrations and share their ideas about these pressure characters as they work through the activity sheet.

What's the goal of these Pressure Characters? (To pressure you to do what they want.) **Do you know anyone who sometimes talks and acts like one of these characters? Even if you have friends like these, you don't need to give into any of their manipulations. But sometimes their use of pressure does work. Why do their schemes work? What are some reasons peer pressure is so powerful?** (We don't recognize it as pressure, we want to belong, we want to be accepted, it hurts when we're put down, we don't want to stick out as a geek or nerd, no one wants to be called *dumb* or *afraid*, we want to be looked up to.) **All of us want to belong and be accepted. Usually it's not much fun to stick out.**

Your power key against peer pressure is our Unit Affirmation: I can learn to think for myself! Display the Unit Affirmation poster and read the Affirmation aloud together. Ask the class to think of a phrase that describes one thing about peer pressure. Choose one similar to "and notice when others put pressure on me." Write the phrase on line one of the poster.

Have you heard about the guy who had to stand up against 400 people at once? He had a lot of peer pressure to deal with in our story from the Bible today.

✔ Searching the Scripture (20 minutes)

Ask for volunteers to read or act the characters in the story. You will need seven individuals and a group to represent 400. (Jehoshaphat, King of Judah; Ahab, King of Israel; Micaiah, a prophet of the true God; a messenger; an Official to the King of Israel; a narrator; Zedekiah, one of the 400 prophets or advisors who didn't follow God.)

> **OPTIONAL:** Have the students set up appropriate props and put on some costumes.

Ask the kids to skim over the story in I Kings 22:1-28 so each character can see what to do and say to make the story come alive. The group of 400 will need to plan their actions together.

Have the narrator begin the story by reading I Kings 22:1-3a, followed by the King of Israel speaking to his official. After the story has been completed, discuss the difficult position of Micaiah.

What did the kings want to have advice about? (Whether it was wise to try to reclaim land that really belonged to them.) Ahab, King of Israel, had already made his plans and wanted God to give His divine OK on them. King Ahab's religious staff of 400 prophets simply restated his desire, hoping to encourage the fulfillment of what Ahab wanted to hear. They gave Ahab the answer he wanted: victory was on the way.

Why do you think King Jehoshaphat wanted an additional response to the question? (King Jehoshaphat wanted true and wise counsel from someone who would speak God's will and plans for the people. He wanted to know and be part of God's plans, the God who really does know the future and what will happen.)

Who was Micaiah? (A prophet of the Lord God, not a member of the religious council serving the king.) **Why did the kings go to him?** (He would ask God for the truth; he wasn't afraid to speak the truth, even if it was bad news for the king.)

What are some of the negative pressures Micaiah encountered? Help the students see that Micaiah may have been intimidated by all the robes and thrones. The crowd of prophets was blowing horns and talking as if they really

did know the true God. Their lies may have been difficult to see through. All the prophets were saying the same thing, "everybody else was saying it." **The messenger was trying to use his influence to help Micaiah. What kind of pressure was that?**

What were the possible dangers to Micaiah with 400 people trying to change his mind? Could he have been hurt physically? Ask for opinions on what might have happened.

What did Micaiah do that shows you he was able to withstand the pressure of a king and more than 400 other people? (He didn't just go along with the gang, he thought for himself, he prayed and listened to God, and made the hard choice to speak whatever God showed him, regardless of the outcome.) Micaiah did not have an easy decision or choice to make, but he didn't let the pressure of others stop him.

Since Micaiah was talking to both kings, was his response in verse 15 accurate? (Yes, they would be victorious in battle.) When King Ahab pressed for details, Micaiah spoke God's word that the people would be left without a shepherd, since King Ahab would be killed.

What do you imagine Micaiah was thinking when he said that the 400 religious leaders were lying, and King Ahab would die? (It was a hard thing to do, yet he knew his God was more powerful than anything and would give the help needed.) Micaiah probably realized that the king could kill him for saying what he said.

Our Unit Verse gives us some instruction about going along with the crowd, or even one other person. Display the Unit Verse and read it together. Distribute large pieces of butcher paper, pencils, and scissors and have the students work together to make individual Unit Verse Patterns. Each student is to make a life–sized silhouette of himself or herself by lying down on the butcher paper and having another student trace around the entire body. Have them cut out their figures and write names on them for identification. Attach the patterns to the walls around the room. Each week in this unit something will be added to the pattern to illustrate *conforming* versus *transforming* words and actions.

✓ Living the Lesson (5-10 minutes)

Distribute copies of the activity sheet "Hidden Pressures" (page 16). Ask students to work together to complete an ending for each story. Then have them find and circle the hidden pressure words used and identify the Pressure Characters.

As time allows, have students think of other situations when they need to be more aware of peer pressure. Refer to the list you made on the chalkboard or poster board. **What are some expressions or words you circled on the activity sheet that indicate unfair pressure?** (Do it for me, everyone who is anyone, what kind of friend are you?)

Distribute balloons and have each student inflate at least one. Working in groups of two or three, tell them to use a marking pen and write on the balloons an expression that sounds like pressure. Talk about the words written on the balloons and why they are able to influence us. Then at a set signal, have everyone either pop the balloons or release the air from the balloons and let them float around the room. **The pressure expressions can't hurt you when they aren't hidden. When you can recognize the pressure for what it is, it can be as meaningless as the air in your balloon.**

Pray together to close the class, asking God to help us see peer pressure for what it is and strengthen us to respond wisely. Offer thanksgiving for the opportunity we have for growth and change as we learn together.

You know the right thing to do, but someone is putting pressure on you to do something else. Identify and match the PRESSURE CHARACTERS with what they might say to influence you to act THEIR way. Find the:

1. (uses a guilt trip)
Victim

2. (uses seduction)
Salesman

3. (uses lies and secrets)
Enemy Agent

4. (uses ultimatum)
Bully

5. (uses imaginary illness)
Sympathy Seeker

6. (uses open manipulation)
Brat

"just one time won't hurt and besides no one will find out; it's not wrong as long as no one catches us."

"how could you do this to me?; If you don't help me I'll . . . flunk, die; If you really liked me, you would . . ."

"go along with what I say because, as you can see, I'm not feeling well."

"here's an offer you just can't refuse . . ."

"do it or I'll . . . beat you up, steal your lunch, spread a lie, tell the teacher or your parents."

"do what I want or I'll . . . get angry, embarrass you, fall apart, won't go, tell . . ."

Hidden Pressures

How do you think this story should end? Write the ending you prefer. Then go back and underline the pressure words and identify the Pressure Character represented.

Everybody is going to the big party after the ball game on Thursday night. Everybody who's anybody is going to be there. You just have to go.

I know and I'm sure it'll be a lot of fun. But I've got a math test on Friday morning. I don't know if it'd be such a great idea to go.

Oh, don't worry. It'll only be this once. What's one test? Besides you've already got a good grade in there. Mrs. Hamilton won't flunk you or anything. Just forget studying and go and have a good time. We'll even go to the mall on Wednesday to shop for an outfit. That's an offer you can't refuse!

But aren't you concerned about your grade? Let's study together on Tuesday and Wednesday. We'll get ready ahead of time, pass the test, and then we can enjoy the party too.

No way. Come to the mall with me on Wednesday, or there's no way I'll go with you to the party Thursday. Ah come on. How could you do this to me? Everybody who's anybody is going to be there and you want me to go without you? What kind of a friend are you? Oh, now you've done it. You've made my stomach start hurting again. Let's do something else right now.

Girl #2: _____

_____

_____

_____

_____

_____

_____

Lesson 2

The Choice Is Yours

Aim: That your students will learn to make wise decisions by considering potential results instead of what others say.

Scripture: Judges 16:4-22

Unit Verse: Do not conform any longer to the pattern of this world, but be transformed by the renewing of your mind. Romans 12:2

Unit Affirmation: I CAN LEARN TO THINK FOR MYSELF!

 Planning Ahead

1. Photocopy Activity Sheets (pages 23 and 24)—one for each student.
2. Write each of these Choice statements on separate pieces of paper: YOU CHOOSE TO HIT BACK, YOU CHOOSE TO WALK AWAY WITHOUT SAYING ANYTHING, YOU CHOOSE TO START YELLING, YOU CHOOSE TO JUST STAND THERE WITHOUT HITTING OR SAYING ANYTHING.
3. Use four 3" x 5" cards to write out the "What Do I Do?" situations as described in LIVING THE LESSON.

 1 **Setting the Stage** (5-10 minutes)

WHAT YOU'LL DO

- Use an activity sheet to write possible consequences
- Play a game to match choices and consequences

WHAT YOU'LL NEED

- "You Choose—It Happens" Activity Sheet (page 23)

2 **Introducing the Issue** (20 minutes)

WHAT YOU'LL DO

- Discuss the chain of consequences that result from a choice
- Add a line to the Unit Affirmation poster

WHAT YOU'LL NEED

- Four Choice statements
- Unit Affirmation poster

3 **Searching the Scriptures** (20 minutes)

WHAT YOU'LL DO

- Use an activity sheet to see one man's consequences
- Write or draw a guideline on the brain of the Unit Verse Pattern

WHAT YOU'LL NEED

- "Samson and Delilah" Activity Sheet (page 24)
- Unit Verse Patterns

 4 **Living the Lesson** (5-10 minutes)

WHAT YOU'LL DO

- Roleplay three different ways to respond to a situation

WHAT YOU'LL NEED

- "What Do I Do?" cards

 # Setting the Stage (5-10 minutes)

As students arrive, give them copies of the activity sheet "You Choose—It Happens" (page 23). Ask them to write possible consequences for at least five of the choices. As needed, discuss a variety of things that could happen in each circumstance emphasizing that each choice we make has at least one consequence. Have the students cut their cards apart and mix them with those of one or more other students to play "Choice and Consequence Memory." On half of the cards should be decisions or choices and the other half has outcomes or consequences.

To play, all the cards are spread out facedown. Each player takes a turn by turning over two of the cards at a time. If the cards match, the player keeps the cards and takes another turn. If the cards do not match, the cards are turned back over and another player takes a turn. The object of the game is to remember which cards have been turned over so when a specific match is needed, the right card can be found. Continue playing until all matches are made or time is up.

We've been playing a game by matching some decisions or choices and their possible outcomes. Most of our consequences don't happen as fast as this game, but it does remind us of what their effect might be.

 # Introducing the Issue (20 minutes)

What choices in the game would be easy for you to make? Allow for responses. **With easy choices, do you even stop to think about the consequences?** Many things happen every day and we just react—we do something without even thinking about it. Talk about some of the automatic things we do every day. (Decide what to wear, walk to school, talk to different people, watch TV.) Many things we do seem to have no consequence, but *every* action does has some effect on someone or something. **What if I skipped breakfast every day, or daydreamed in class, or made a smart remark back to someone or watched TV every day? What might be the consequences of these things that may seem so unimportant?**

What about some of the harder choices in the game? Which ones are those? Discuss the choices we can make before a situation comes to such a difficult place. Sometimes our choices keep us from needing to make other decisions.

Making decisions, whether they seem major or minor, is an important

part of everyday life for us. What can we do to make the best decisions we can? (Consider what the possible consequences might be, ask friends or trusted adults what they've done or would do, study the Bible, ask God to guide us.)

When you're making choices, do you think through what the outcome of those choices might be? Explain that sometimes we are able to take the time to seriously think through things, and other times we're not. Sometimes things just seem to happen, and we *go with the flow* based on who we are without thinking through to the outcome. This may not always be bad, as in the case with the physical body reflexes God has given to each of us, or jumping out of the way of a car with squealing brakes.

Divide the class into four teams and give each team one of the Choice statements described in Planning Ahead. **You are in a difficult situation. Something has just happened, such as a call made at the ball game you are playing. Everyone seems to be arguing about what is right but some of them think you are at fault. What are you going to do?** Talk about how many different choices we have even when we don't realize it, and each of those choices may have a different consequence. Each consequence may then mean another choice with a different consequence, and this can continue on. Have the teams talk about the Choice statement they have and decide what a possible consequence could be if they actually made that choice in the above situation. Ask them to go one step further and decide what the next choice and the next consequence might be and whether these are wise choices.

> **OPTIONAL:** Have each team act out the situation and the choice represented on its card. Encourage the team to take it further to the next choices that will be made.

Sometimes our decisions about what choices to make are based on what we think *might* happen, instead of our really knowing what would happen. What would you do differently in some of these choices if you knew for sure what the consequences would be?

Which of the choices we've been talking about have ended up with a good or positive outcome? As the students mention those that are good, or positive, begin a list on the chalkboard or a poster board. Put a plus sign at the top of the list. **If a different choice was made, how could the outcome have been different, either positive or negative?**

Display the Unit Affirmation poster and read it aloud together. Ask the class to think of a phrase that describes something about peer pressure and choices.

Choose one similar to "by first thinking about the consequences of my actions." Write the selected phrase on line two of the poster.

One person in the Bible who had a difficult time considering the results of his choices was Samson. He had a number of opportunities to learn to think ahead, but he chose what he thought was the fun of the moment.

 # Searching the Scripture (20 minutes)

Samson was dedicated to God as a Nazirite from his birth, which meant he was set apart to God. One symbol of this Nazirite commitment was that he wouldn't shave the hair on his head. Although he was dedicated to God and God gave him exceptional physical strength, Samson consistently had problems thinking about the consequences of his actions.

Samson's strength was well known in the city of Gaza. The local people, the Philistines, knew that Samson had caught and torn apart an attacking lion, killed a thousand of the enemy army at one time, ripped off metal bonds with his bare hands, and pulled the giant door of the city with the two gateposts, bar and all, out of the ground, then carried all of it to the top of a hill 30 miles away. The Philistines were a group of people who did not serve God and were fighting with God's people. They admired Samson for his strength, but since he was an enemy, they wanted to find out how he could be so strong so they could take his strength away. Obviously, Samson would not let his enemies know the source of his strength, but he had to withstand a lot of pressure to keep from telling them.

As we read the story, listen for the source of Samson's strength. Also, listen for the times when he had a choice to make. Each time Samson has a choice, we'll stop the reading and all of you move to one side of the room. While you are there, we'll talk about what you think Samson's choice should be.

Have students read Judges 16:4-22, but change readers and stop to discuss Samson's choice after verses six, ten, thirteen, and seventeen. Ask the students to move to a different part of the room every time Samson had an opportunity to make a choice. After the story is completed, talk about Samson's choices and his pressure.

How many times did Samson have an opportunity to make a new choice? (Four.) **Doesn't it seem like he would have reconsidered before it was too late? Most of us don't have that many chances to make the same choice.**

Why didn't he leave or make a different choice? (He didn't want to lose Delilah, he didn't think it would hurt to play a game, he didn't think through the consequences of his choice but just did what he wanted at the moment.) **What was the source of Samson's strength?** (Power of the Spirit of God, his obedience to God and staying faithful to his Nazirite promise.) **To whom did Samson listen?** (Not to God but to Delilah who persistently pestered him and manipulated him with many types of pressures.) **What happened when he listened to others instead of considering the possible results of his choices?** (He lied several times, eventually told his secret.) Samson got in deeper and deeper, and he continued to stay in the bad situation with peers who weren't influencing him for good. He forgot about God and finally broke his promise of silence and spilled the secret of his strength.

Samson did not think for himself. He foolishly listened to others and did not consider the possible results of his choices. We are going to do a rap based on this story of Samson, Delilah, and the Philistines. Distribute copies of the activity sheet "Samson and Delilah" (page 24). You may want to give the students a chance to read silently through the activity sheet before it is read as a class. Ask for volunteers to read these parts: Samson, Philistines (two or more people), Delilah, Rhythm (a small group or the rest of the class). After the rap is presented, talk about Samson's advice. **How did Samson yield to pressure?** (Listened to the pressure of Delilah rather than to God, he stayed around bad influences rather than leaving, he did not pray to ask for God's help.) **What advice does Samson give you in this rap?**

Read the Unit Verse together. Discuss what the students could write or draw on the brain of their Unit Verse Pattern. **Not thinking about the consequences is one way we conform to the pattern of this world. What guideline can you write that would show you have chosen to follow God's pattern instead?** Have the kids write a statement or two on the brains of their patterns, such as "I'll think first instead of just going along." If you prefer, have the guidelines written on a Post-it type note and attached to the head of the pattern.

Living the Lesson (5-10 minutes)

Before class, write each of these "What Do I Do?" situations on separate 3" x 5" cards.

1. You forgot to get information on a current event for class; now the teacher's giving a pop quiz and you have to write the details. What do you do?

2. Your friends are going to a party, but the hosting friend's parents are out

of town. Your family rule is you don't go to anyone's house unless an adult is present. What do you do?

3. Your best friend rented your favorite video and you watched it together last night, and he forgot to do the math homework. The substitute wants to collect it and your friend wants to copy your work. What do you do?

4. The most popular guy in school is at your table for lunch and has brought an alcoholic cooler. Your best friend doesn't want to drink it, but everyone is taking a sip. What do you do?

What words were repeated in the Samson rap? ("I can think for myself. I'll think it through! You can think for yourself. Just think it through!") **Do you think of what the consequences might be when you make choices? Sometimes it isn't easy to think through all the possible consequences, but it is important. Even when we don't stop to think about the choices that are there. For example, when someone says something to you, you even have a choice about what to say back.**

Divide the class into four teams and give each team one of the 3" x 5" cards. Ask the teams to discuss three different choices to respond to their situation and then act out each one to the rest of the class. As time permits, discuss the consequences after each team has presented its choices.

Close in prayer, thanking God for the ability He gives us to think about our choices. Express your love for God and the members of the group.

You Choose — It Happens

All choices bring consequences, sometimes more than one! What are the consequences of the choices listed here? Fill in some consequences that could happen if you made these choices, then write your own CHOICE and CONSEQUENCE cards. Cut the cards apart, mix them with the other player's cards and consider all the consequences!

CHOICE You choose to overeat on a regular basis.	**CHOICE** You choose to practice basketball every day.	**CHOICE** You choose to not stop your bicycle at a red light.
CONSEQUENCE _____ _____ _____	**CONSEQUENCE** _____ _____ _____	**CONSEQUENCE** _____ _____ _____
CHOICE You choose to study for a test.	**CHOICE** You choose to stay up late on a school night to watch a video.	**CHOICE** You choose to save the money you earned doing yard work.
CONSEQUENCE _____ _____ _____	**CONSEQUENCE** _____ _____ _____	**CONSEQUENCE** _____ _____ _____
CHOICE You choose to cheat on your homework.	**CHOICE** You choose to be a good friend in a difficult situation.	**CHOICE** You choose to take some clothes from a store without paying.
CONSEQUENCE _____ _____ _____	**CONSEQUENCE** _____ _____ _____	**CONSEQUENCE** _____ _____ _____

CHOICE _____ _____ _____	**CONSEQUENCE** _____ _____ _____

 # Samson and Delilah

SAMSON: My name is Samson and I'm here to say
That following God is the only way. When folks come and tell you something to do, You'd better think through what you're going to do. Once I went to Gaza, where Delilah I saw.
She didn't love God; her reputation was raw. But I didn't care. I didn't think it through long. It seemed like fun. I didn't care it was wrong.

RHYTHM: I can think for myself. I'll think it through! You can think for yourself. Just think it through!

SAMSON: I listened to Delilah, her wish was my law. I forgot God and promises, it was fun that I saw.

RHYTHM: I can think for myself. I'll think it through! You can think for yourself too.

PHILISTINES: We Philistines went to Delilah and said, "You can get the strength secret right out of his head. We'll overcome Samson and tie him down,
And your pay will be silver. How's 28 pounds!"

DELILAH: Well the offer was rich and I wanted the money
So I quickly said "Yes!" Then I went to my honey, "Tell the secret of your strength, say only what's true. Samson, how can you be tied up and subdued?"

RHYTHM: I can think for myself. I'll think it through! You can think for yourself, too.

SAMSON: Oh I'm sorry to say that I didn't do good
For I didn't say "No", "Why?", or do what I should. So I stayed right there, I didn't think it through, And to the pressure gave in; told a big untruth.

DELILAH: "The Philistines are here, Samson!" I cried,
Not knowing that of his strength's source he'd lied. But he snapped through the thongs as if they were string. They didn't weaken Samson—didn't do anything!

RHYTHM: I can think for myself. I'll think it through! You can think for yourself, too.

SAMSON: You might be thinking now the pressure would be growing
From Delilah of my strength's source to be knowing. Oh she did not give up. I tried another whopper. She kept on and on. Nothing would stop her. The game was out of hand. It was no longer fun. I knew not what to say, though something must be done. Though God had told me "No!" I told her the whole story
Of my hair and being sacred to God's glory.

RHYTHM: I can think for myself. I'll think it through! You can think for yourself, too!

DELILAH: Yes I listened very well. He told me everything. Then I sent the message back to the ruling Philistines, "Come back here once more and bring my bag of silver! It's time the deed was done. I'm ready to deliver."

RHYTHM: I can think for myself. I'll think it through! You can think for yourself, too!

DELILAH: When Samson was snoring, asleep in my lap, I called the barber, a helpful little chap. He shaved the vital hair right off Samson's head. This time the strength was gone. It left just like he'd said.

SAMSON: I thought of my hair as having "magic" length. I'd forgotten that God was the source of my strength. Sadly I didn't know that God had departed. My commitment to Him was where it all started. I disobeyed God and didn't think at all. The result of my goof was my whole life's flaw. Don't fall into that trap, lose your freedom or sight. Don't give up your life. Think it through. Do right!

RHYTHM: I can think for myself. I'll think it through! You can think for yourself, too!

Lesson 3

A Different Approach

Aim: That your students will learn techniques they can use to reverse negative peer pressure and still keep their friends.

Scripture: I Samuel 24:1-22

Unit Verse: Do not conform any longer to the pattern of this world, but be transformed by the renewing of your mind. Romans 12:2

Unit Affirmation: I CAN LEARN TO THINK FOR MYSELF!

 Planning Ahead

1. Photocopy Activity Sheets (pages 31 and 32)—one for each student.
2. Make a Destination Box by using a large empty rectangular box or trash can. Cover or decorate the box as desired.

1 Setting the Stage (5-10 minutes)

WHAT YOU'LL DO

- Write or draw situations with potential peer pressure
- Design one or more gliders or planes

WHAT YOU'LL NEED

- colorful 8 1/2 x 11 paper—at least two per student

2 Introducing the Issue (20 minutes)

WHAT YOU'LL DO

- Use an activity sheet to identify some tools to resist negative pressure
- Add a line to the Unit Affirmation poster

WHAT YOU'LL NEED

- "You're Stronger than the Pressure" Activity Sheet (page 31)
- Unit Affirmation poster

3 Searching the Scriptures (20 minutes)

WHAT YOU'LL DO

- Use an activity sheet to see how harmful influences can change
- Write or draw a guideline on the arms of the Unit Verse Patterns

WHAT YOU'LL NEED

- "David Resists Pressure" Activity Sheet (page 32)
- Unit Verse Patterns

4 Living the Lesson (5-10 minutes)

WHAT YOU'LL DO

- Give a suggestion of how to turn pressure around

WHAT YOU'LL NEED

- Gliders and planes from SETTING THE STAGE
- Destination Box

Lesson 3

Peer Pressure

✓ Setting the Stage (5-10 minutes)

As the students arrive, give each student two pieces of brightly colored 8 1/2" x 11" paper. Have them fold each in half lengthwise. Ask your students to draw or write on each piece of paper a few sentences about a situation describing someone who doesn't want to do what the group has suggested. Some suggestions might include playing a game, lying, going to the mall, trading assigned seats, copying homework.

When two different situations have been written or drawn, explain that each paper is to be made into a glider or airplane, the more unusual the better. **These flying machines will be tested later, they are just to be created and housed in the Destination Box now.** Have each completed glider be put in the box without being tested. As time allows, more airplanes may be made as long as each one has a different situation noted on it.

There are lots of times you may not want to do what others are doing. Sometimes it may be you'd just rather do something else. Other times it may be that, when you think through it, you figure out that someone is trying to put negative pressure on you. Today we're going to discover some tools we can use to handle the pressure others try to dish out.

✓ Introducing the Issue (20 minutes)

There are many ways to handle the negative peer pressure you find around you. First, you have to realize that it is pressure and then you need to think through what to do next. Mention the four tools for the "what to do next" part of the challenge. These are: an answering machine, a key to escape a trap, lips, and a Bible.

What does an answering machine do? (Helps to get a message to some-one else, gives the same message over and over again.) **Imagine someone calls you and tries to pressure you to go with him when you have other things to do. Turn on your answering machine tool by saying your decision to the caller. No matter how much you're pressured, your answering machine says the same thing.** Choose two students to roleplay the above-mentioned situation. Discuss whether the answering machine tool would be effective as a response to pressure.

Our second tool is used to help us escape a trap. What do you think of when you look at a trap? (It's ready to catch someone, pain of getting caught, it's out of sight but very effective in catching what's not wanted.) **We**

26

need a tool to help us against traps that we may not know about, such as when someone is lying and trying to deceive. Our tool against the trap is a "key" which represents prayer. Prayer is available faster than anything. We can ask God for help to know what to do in a split–second prayer. Prayer can keep us from traps and can help us respond by saying, "What you're telling me is a trap of lies and secrets just waiting to catch someone; that trap will spring sometime, maybe this time or maybe later, but lies and secrets are a habit that I don't even want to start."

Our next tool is lips, perhaps the most popular tool being widely used today. What's the slogan for the anti-drug campaign? (Just say *no*.) Imagine that someone is trying to convince you of how innocent something is. Using the lips tool you tell her, "See my lips? Nnnnooo; I will not give in to the pressure." What else could you say with your lips to turn the pressure around? (I can live without that, and so can you; what you're selling me isn't something I'm going to buy into.).

The fourth tool is the one that is always present and backs up the other tools. This is the tool that says, "God is my strength and my guide. I will not give in to pressures to do wrong or follow anyone other than God." This final tool is God's Word, the Bible that teaches us of God's power to fight our battles for us. God has promised in His Word to take care of us as we trust our lives to Him.

When are some appropriate times to use these tools to help you with negative peer pressure? Distribute copies of the activity sheet "You're Stronger than the Pressure" (page 31). As the kids are working on this, discuss other times than those listed when each tool is needed.

Display the Unit Affirmation poster and read it aloud together. Ask the class to think of a phrase to add to the poster. Choose one similar to "and turn negative peer pressure around to my own good." Write the selected phrase on line three of the poster.

Our Bible story is about a man who faced a strong pressure character and used one of today's tools to help. He had a great opportunity to take the easy way out, but resisted peer pressure, and even turned the pressure around for good!

✓ Searching the Scripture (20 minutes)

David is the person who had to face extreme pressure from King Saul and at times his own friends. This event took place in and near a cave

where David was hiding with about 400 supporters. See I Samuel 22:1, 2. Have students take turns reading the story in I Samuel 24:1-22, but stop the reading after verse four. **David's friends were trying to convince him that it was the right time to act. What kind of pressure did they put on David?** (Negative: "Here's an offer you can't refuse." They were lying and deceiving. "Just this time it's okay. This is what God spoke of.") **After listening to his men, what is the first thing David did?** (He cut off some of Saul's robe, he didn't stop to think, he showed off.)

Ask the students to continue reading through verse seven. **What was David's first clue that he'd given into negative pressure?** (He felt guilty, was conscience-stricken.) **When David felt guilty, what did he do?** (He stopped, he realized he'd blown it and just reacted to what the others said, instead of thinking for himself.) **Can you find an example when David listened to God and said "No"?** (In verse 6 David said, "The Lord forbid that I should do such a thing.")

David had blown it, but he didn't give up. When he felt guilty and realized his mistake, he started thinking through things and using some tools to help him. Have the students read the rest of the story.

In verses 6 and 7, David turned the pressure around and used his influence on his friends. What tool did he use? (His words [lips] to say "no" and explain why Saul should not be harmed.) David explained his faith in God as the true authority. He knew it wasn't his place to harm Saul, even though Saul wasn't doing the right thing. Talk about how difficult it is to leave a situation alone, especially when we know we are in the right.

Saul heard David explain his innocence and questions about being hunted. What could have happened if Saul were still angry? Discuss the students' opinions of how this story could have ended differently. Talk about the frustration or attitudes when we *can't* explain how we feel or talk about why we are doing something different from the crowd. **What was Saul's response to David in verse 17?** (He realized that David had treated him kindly, even though Saul wasn't doing the right thing.) It takes strength, wise choices, and determination to be like David and handle pressure by turning away from it.

Have teams look for places in the story when David used specific tools for help. As mentioned, David used the *lips* tool when he said "No" in verse six. Have one team look for a use of the *answering machine* tool. (Reason of his decision and turning the pressure around: verses 8-11, 14) Ask the second team to look for *Bible* and *key* (prayer) tools. (Puts it in God's hands: verses 12, 13, 15.)

Distribute the activity sheet, "David Resists Pressure" (page 32). Give the students time to complete the grid and then place the words in the statements at the bottom of the page. Answers are: 1. <u>Listen</u> to what people are <u>saying</u>. 2. Think through the <u>pressure</u> they're trying to use. 3. Be aware of <u>feelings</u> such as guilt, fear, anger. 4. <u>Confess</u> wrongdoing and ask <u>forgiveness</u>. 5. Explain <u>choice</u> and <u>decision</u> to others. 6. Give an <u>alternative</u>. 7. Ask God to <u>avenge</u> any wrongdoing.

What are the seven things listed on the activity sheet that help us to follow David's example? Ask several students to participate in reading the statements and giving examples of each one.

Read the Unit Verse together. Discuss what words of advice the students could write on the arms of their Unit Verse Pattern. **When we just go along with the crowd, we conform to the pattern of this world. What guideline can you write or draw that would show you have chosen to follow God's pattern instead?** Have the kids write a statement or two on the arms of their patterns, such as "I'll ask God to help me know what to do when I see negative pressure around." If you prefer, have the students decorate the part of the pattern that is being used each week.

✓ Living the Lesson (5-10 minutes)

Have the students form three teams and set up the room so the gliders from SETTING THE STAGE can be tested. Place the Destination Box on its side with the open end facing three chairs put side by side about 9—12 feet away (across the room).

As the gliders are retrieved from their earlier storage place and the teams are moving into position behind each team chair, discuss some possible responses the students could give to help turn the pressure situations around. For example, saying "no," encouraging others to come with you, discussing consequences, getting advice from a trusted adult, offering a better or different idea.

Three pilots, one from each team, will test a glider at the same time. The pilot's challenge is to first think of a way to turn the negative peer pressure described on the glider into a positive one. After the three seated pilots have described the written situation and described a "turn around," at the signal, the gliders are flown to the Destination Box. Choose one starting pilot for each team and begin the challenge. You may want to set aside the gliders that make it into or in front of the box and have a final challenge round with those.

Of all the pressure situations we've just talked about, which ones are

the hardest to turn around? When is it better to just stop and not try to change things? Allow for responses. **Saying no and walking away can be a hard thing to do, but there may be times when it might be the best choice.**

Close with a prayer of thankfulness that God wants to guide us in all our choices and ask for help in the decisions to be made in the coming week. Pray for the friends outside this class who also need to learn to handle peer pressure.

You're Stronger than the Pressure

You have been given several tools to help you with the pressure characters. Choose which tool(s) you would use in the following situations and draw or write it in the box.

A. "How could you do this to me? If you don't help me I'll flunk. If you really liked me you would give me the answers."

———————————
———————————
———————————

B. "I know you aren't supposed to go there, but if you go with me, you can use my roller blades."

———————————
———————————
———————————

C. "Just one time won't hurt and besides no one will find out; it's not wrong as long as no one sees us."

———————————
———————————
———————————

D. "Go with me or I'll tell the teacher you cheated on that last test."

———————————
———————————
———————————

THE TOOLS ARE . . .

ANSWERING MACHINE: Gives the same message over and over. "No, I won't rescue you. (I won't let you copy my homework just because you forgot yours.) No, I won't give in."

KEY (Prayer): Asks God to keep you from falling into a trap, reminds us that God is always with us. "That's just a trap of lies and secrets, and I won't get caught in it. God is greater than anything, and He'll help me say NO to your trap."

LIPS: Say the words that strengthen our thoughts. "See my lips? Nnnnoooo; now let's practice saying it together, 'No!'; I will not give in to your pressure."

BIBLE: Gives instruction about good choices. "I will not follow anyone other than God. I'll be faithful to Him and He will take the best care of me.

David Resists Pressure

Fill in the grid with the following words. "Choice" is entered to help you get started. Then, use the words to complete the statements at the bottom of the page.

6 letters
Avenge
Choice
Listen
Saying

7 letters
Confess

8 letters
Decision
Feelings
Pressure

11 letters
Alternative
Forgiveness

C H O I C E

Like David, we can turn away from pressure if we . . .

1. _____ to what people are _____.

2. Think through the _____ they're trying to use.

3. Be aware of _____ such as guilt, fear, anger.

4. _____ wrongdoing and ask _____.

5. Explain _____ and _____ to others.

6. Give an _____.

7. Ask God to _____ any wrongdoing.

Lesson 4

United We Stand

Aim: That your students will discover methods to help them maintain positive decision-making skills.

Scripture: Numbers 13:16-19, 26-30; 14:22-24; Joshua 1:1-9

Unit Verse: Do not conform any longer to the pattern of this world, but be transformed by the renewing of your mind.
Romans 12:2

Unit Affirmation: I CAN LEARN TO THINK FOR MYSELF!

 Planning Ahead

1. Photocopy Activity Sheets (pages 39 and 40)—one for each student.
2. Prepare the Word Clues by writing these words on colored 3" x 5" cards or paper. Make duplicates of cards as necessary so each student will have one card. Write these words on green cards: ALIVE, GREY, STRONG. On red cards: ANIMAL, ZOO, CIRCUS. On blue cards: AFRICAN, INDIAN, EARS.
3. Tie seven to ten long (fireplace) wooden matches in a bundle.
4. Write the Bible references and questions on a chalkboard or poster board as described in SEARCHING THE SCRIPTURES.

 Setting the Stage (5-10 minutes)

WHAT YOU'LL DO

• Play Word Clues to demonstrate working together

WHAT YOU'LL NEED

• Word Clues cards

2 **Introducing the Issue** (20 minutes)

WHAT YOU'LL DO

• Demonstrate the value of sticking together
• Use an activity sheet to talk about benefits of support groups
• Add a line to the Unit Affirmation poster

WHAT YOU'LL NEED

• A bundle of long wooden matches
• "Code of Friendship" Activity Sheet (page 39)
• Unit Affirmation poster

 Searching the Scriptures (20 minutes)

WHAT YOU'LL DO

• Use an activity sheet to learn how friends can help each other
• Write or draw a guideline on the legs of the Unit Verse Patterns

WHAT YOU'LL NEED

• "The Promised Land Press" Activity Sheet (page 40)
• Unit Verse Patterns

 Living the Lesson (5-10 minutes)

WHAT YOU'LL DO

• Create an example of handling pressure together
• Write a reminder card of one way to help a friend this week

WHAT YOU'LL NEED

• 3" x 5" cards—one for each student

☑ Setting the Stage (5-10 minutes)

As students arrive, give each one a Word Clue card. Tell them that the cards contain clues to help identify something and their task is to solve the puzzle by using as few Word Clues as possible. Students may check with others having the same color card. If the puzzle is still unsolved, have them check with students having clues of one other color. Continue to expand the clues available with the other color cards until the answer is identified. (The answer is: elephant.)

With these Word Clues you didn't have enough information to figure out the answer until you worked together. Many of the things we do are improved as we work or play with a friend. We may make better decisions and get more accomplished, and we also can provide that same help for others.

☑ Introducing the Issue (20 minutes)

Here is another example. If one of you tried to use your hands to break this bundle do you think you could break it? Put the bundle of wooden matches where it can be seen by everyone and have one student try to break it. **Could two of you working together use your hands to break this bundle?** Let two students try to break the bundle of matches. **This bundle is just like us. When we stick together and help each other, we stay strong and the peer pressure will not be able to break us.** Unwrap the bundle and begin breaking the matches one at a time. **When we try to stand without the help of others, it's much easier to be broken by the pressure and not think through to the consequences.**

Have you ever had to do something really frightening or difficult? Have a few students briefly describe their experiences for the group. **Did you ask a friend to help you or come along with you? If so, did that make it easier? In what way did it make the situation different?** (We had more ideas together, it was more fun, it felt good to have "moral support" and to know someone cared or was praying for me.) Sometimes it does not change things, but the positive support from a friend goes a long way and means a lot. Other times it actually changes the situation! Sometimes it is lots of fun; other times it takes effort.

What are some ways friends have helped you? Allow for responses. **Can you think of ways you help your friends?** Allow for responses. **The things**

we've been talking about are what are often called "support groups." Support groups help influence each other in positive ways. The purpose of a support group is to support, to help, care, encourage, and do this by being available and trustworthy.

All that support begins with friendship and being a friend. There are many stories about friendship in the Bible. The words *friends* and *friendship* are mentioned over 100 times in the Bible. There are some biblical and general ways that teach us about being a good friend, to use positive pressures, and to be a part of helpful support groups. Distribute copies of the activity sheet "Code of Friendship" (page 39). **Here are some keys for building friendships and positive support groups. It's your mission to crack the code.** The answers are: 1. Be a friend and make a friend. 2. Choose friends who will help you in positive ways. 3. Be willing to talk about what you are thinking and feeling. 4. Encourage others to share their thoughts with you. 5. Help others by offering your friendship. 6. Remember others are just as scared or nervous as you are. 7. Ask questions they cannot answer with yes or no. 8. Show you are interested in them. 9. Continue to be willing to stand alone. 10. Pray.

Have the students solve the puzzles and then discuss their reactions to the statements in the code. **Are there any you would change? Why?** Encourage a variety of attitudes about friendship. A good way to make a new friend is by taking the initiative; don't always wait for someone to come to you. Choose to hang out with friends who are the kind of people you want to be like.

Display the Unit Affirmation poster and read it aloud together. Ask the class to think of a phrase that describes using peer pressure wisely. Choose one similar to "to make good decisions and use them to help someone else." Write the selected phrase on line four of the poster.

Friends can help each other in all kinds of situations, including standing against negative influences. Our story is about two friends who needed all the support they could get.

✓ Searching the Scripture (20 minutes)

Before class, write these Bible references and questions on the chalkboard or a poster board.

1. Read Numbers 13:16-33; 14:21-24; Joshua 1:1-9.
2. What does Numbers 13:17-20 say the spy team is to do?
3. What does Caleb say about going into the land?

4. What does God say about Caleb's attitude and spirit?

5. Why would following God "wholeheartedly" make a difference to God?

6. What does Joshua 1:8 say we are to do with the Bible?

7. What was to be the source of Joshua's strength and courage?

Two friends who had learned the benefit of helping each other were Caleb and Joshua. They were Israelites who had been with Moses and they had been through some interesting times together. Explain that Caleb and Joshua's earlier experiences included being delivered from Pharaoh and slavery in Egypt, seeing the Red Sea parted, and being fed with food (manna) that God sent from the sky.

At the time of our story, Caleb and Joshua are chosen to be two members of a spy team sent by Moses (by God's command) to explore the land of Canaan. Canaan was the land they would be moving to. God had promised it to Israel, but the spy team was to get an advance look.

Distribute copies of activity sheet, "The Promised Land Press," (page 40.) Have all the students read the verses listed on the chalkboard or poster board. Form four groups and give the first group question #2 and have the students write a news article answering that question under the headline, "Spies Sent on Mission." Give the second group question #3 and have those students write a news article under the headline, "Caleb: Crazy or Courageous?" Give the third group questions 4 and 5 and have the kids write an article under the headline, "God Rewards Wholehearted Effort." Finally, give the fourth group questions 6 and 7 and have those students write an article under the headline, "Joshua Finds Source of Courage." After the articles have been written have each group read its story.

What was the report brought back by the spy team? (It's a rich land, lots of food, people are powerful, cities are large.) **What is the thinking of most of the spies regarding the land and people?** (The spies were afraid to go into the land because the people were so powerful.) **Did everyone on the Spy Team give the same report?** (No.)

Why was Caleb's response to the report different than most of the others'? (He believed God's promise about giving them the land, the others didn't think it through and just saw the problem, they didn't remember God's promise and power.)

Joshua and Caleb stood together and told the people that God would lead them into the land and give it to them. God honored their faith by allowing them to be part of those who later settled the land. What is the difference between being *wholehearted* or *halfhearted* about something? Could this make a difference when you have to make a decision?

Lesson 4

See that all the questions on the chalkboard or poster board have been answered and then focus on Joshua 1:1-9. **If the Lord your God is with you *wherever* you go, what is your source of courage for standing up to others when you need to?** Ask the students to find the number of times they are reminded in these verses to be strong and courageous. Discuss the other guidelines also written there.

Joshua and Caleb gave each other help and positive pressure when the other spies were against them. Because of the faith they shared, and the way they supported each other, God gave them a special blessing. Even two people can make a mini-support group!

Read the Unit Verse together and distribute the Unit Verse Patterns. Discuss what transforming words from this lesson can be written on the legs of their patterns. Have the kids write a statement or two on their patterns, such as "I'll make decisions that can help someone else." If you prefer, have the kids discuss a contrast and write both a conforming statement and a transforming statement, such as, "hurting others doesn't matter" versus "I'm proud to be kind and gentle to others." If possible in your room, attach the Unit Verse Patterns to the wall in such a way that they are joining hands as a symbol of support and help.

✔ Living the Lesson (5-10 minutes)

Here's a way to help you remember that we can handle pressure better as we work together. Explain that the group is going to make a "Standing Circle Seat." Ask the students to form a circle, and then turn to the right to look at the back of someone's head. Have the kids tighten the circle by moving in very close to each other and then slowly bend their knees until they are sitting down on the lap of the person behind them. **This is positive pressure working together.**

Today we've talked a lot about friendship, encouragement, and positive support groups. Are there some things we can *do* to help our friends? Talk about some things that could be done this week to show support and encouragement. For example, be willing to listen and not laugh, share own experiences and feelings, encourage to talk when "down," ask if he or she needs help. **What kinds of things would be helpful to you if you were the one needing support?** (Listen to me, do things together, have the other person make the first move to see if I'm okay.) **What things should**

people *not* do? (Not tease or make fun, not talk about you to others.)

Distribute 3" x 5" cards and pencils and ask the kids to write themselves a confidential note about who to help and support this week. **What is one specific thing you can do, or not do, to encourage a certain person?** Encourage the students to take the cards home and use them as a reminder that they can help others stand against negative influences.

Close in prayer, asking God for help and courage to do the things we have written on our reminders. Express thanks for God's example of love for us and the privilege of sharing that love with others through friendships.

Here are some important steps to building friendships and support groups. Unfortunately there has been a problem with the computer. Can you help decode the words and write them as they should be?

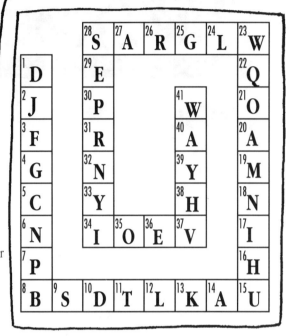

1. Be a __ __ __ __ __ __ and __ __ __ __ a friend.
   3 31 34 29 32 1   19 40 13 36

2. __ __ __ __ __ __ friends who will __ __ __ __ you in
   5 16 35 21 9 36   16 29 12 30
   __ __ __ __ __ __ __ __ ways.
   30 21 9 17 11 17 37 36

3. Be __ __ __ __ __ __ __ to __ __ __ __ about what you are
   23 17 12 12 17 32 25   11 14 12 13
   __ __ __ __ __ __ __ and __ __ __ __ __ __ __ .
   11 38 34 6 13 34 6 25   3 36 36 24 34 32 25

4. __ __ __ __ __ __ __ __ __ others to __ __ __ __ __ their
   36 6 5 21 15 31 40 25 36   9 16 20 31 29
   __ __ __ __ __ __ __ __ with you.
   11 38 35 15 25 38 11 9

5. __ __ __ __ others by __ __ __ __ __ __ __ __ __ your
   38 36 12 30   21 3 3 36 31 17 32 25
   __ __ __ __ __ __ __ __ __ __ .
   3 26 34 36 6 1 28 16 34 30

6. __ __ __ __ __ __ __ __ others are just as __ __ __ __ __ __ or
   31 36 19 36 19 8 36 31   28 5 20 26 36 1
   __ __ __ __ __ __ __ as you are.
   6 29 31 37 21 15 28

7. __ __ __ questions they cannot __ __ __ __ __ __ with __ __ __ or no.
   40 9 13   40 18 9 23 29 31   39 29 9

8. Show you are __ __ __ __ __ __ __ __ __ __ in them.
   34 18 11 29 26 29 9 11 29 1

9. __ __ __ __ __ __ __ __ to be __ __ __ __ __ __ __ to stand
   5 21 32 11 17 32 15 29   23 17 12 12 17 32 25
   __ __ __ __ __ .
   14 12 21 32 29

10. __ __ __ __ .
    30 31 40 39

Code table:
28 S, 27 A, 26 R, 25 G, 24 L, 23 W
1 D, 29 E, 22 Q
2 J, 30 P, 41 W, 21 O
3 F, 31 R, 40 A, 20 A
4 G, 32 N, 39 Y, 19 M
5 C, 33 Y, 38 H, 18 N
6 N, 34 I, 35 O, 36 E, 37 V, 17 I
7 P, 16 H
8 B, 9 S, 10 D, 11 T, 12 L, 13 K, 14 A, 15 U

 # The Promised Land Press

The Promised Land Press

Five Shekels

Spies Sent on Mission

_____
_____
_____
_____
_____
_____
_____
_____
_____
_____

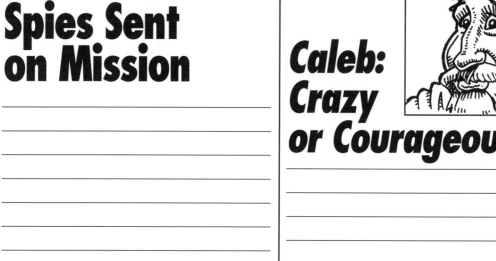

Caleb: Crazy or Courageous?

_____
_____
_____
_____
_____
_____
_____
_____
_____
_____
_____

Joshua Finds Source of Courage

_____
_____
_____
_____
_____

God Rewards Wholehearted Effort

_____
_____
_____
_____
_____

Canaan Weather:
Monday: Hot
Tuesday: Extra Hot
Wednesday: Very Hot

Index

Editorial
Comics

TV/Movies
Sports
Advice

That's What Friends Are For

Aim: That your students will understand that real friends care about each other and use positive methods to influence others to follow God's ways.

Scripture: Daniel 1:8-20

Unit Verse: Do not conform any longer to the pattern of this world, but be transformed by the renewing of your mind.
Romans 12:2

Unit Affirmation: I CAN LEARN TO THINK FOR MYSELF!

 Planning Ahead

1. Photocopy Activity Sheets (pages 47 and 48)—one for each student.
2. Prepare a Friends Graffiti Wall by writing these statements on the top of an 18" x 36" strip of paper: A FRIEND IS . . ., A FRIEND IS NOT . . . . Attach this paper to the wall so it is convenient for writing.
3. Use five 3" x 5" cards or paper to make Challenge cards as described in LIVING THE LESSON.

 Setting the Stage (5-10 minutes)

WHAT YOU'LL DO

* Describe qualities desirable or undesirable in a friend

WHAT YOU'LL NEED

* Friends Graffiti Wall

2 Introducing the Issue (20 minutes)

WHAT YOU'LL DO

* Play a game with an activity sheet to find out interesting facts
* Use an activity sheet to understand how friends care enough to help
* Complete the Unit Affirmation poster

WHAT YOU'LL NEED

* "Autograph Bingo" Activity Sheet (page 47)
* "Superstar Friends" Activity Sheet (page 48)
* Unit Affirmation poster

 Searching the Scriptures (20 minutes)

WHAT YOU'LL DO

* Complete an activity sheet to show how friends direct others to God
* Write or draw a guideline on the heart of the Unit Verse Patterns

WHAT YOU'LL NEED

* "Superstar Friends" Activity Sheet (page 48)
* Unit Verse Patterns

 Living the Lesson (5-10 minutes)

WHAT YOU'LL DO

* Roleplay ways to influence others to follow God's ways

WHAT YOU'LL NEED

* "As a Friend, I Would . . ." Challenge cards

Lesson 5

Setting the Stage (5-10 minutes)

As students arrive, call their attention to the Friends Graffiti Wall. Ask them to write or draw a response to the statements about the qualities they think are important for friends to have or not have. **What are some of the things you value the most in your friends? What kinds of things would stop you from having someone as a friend? Put as many of these characteristics as you can think of on the graffiti wall for our discussion.** Have the students talk about what may bother them about friends and about the things they enjoy. Encourage each one to put several things on the graffiti wall.

Friends are a very important part of our lives. We'll be talking about how friends show they care about each other, and ways true friends can help others follow God.

Introducing the Issue (20 minutes)

How would you describe the best kind of friend you can think of? Allow the students to respond. **Do you agree with the words and pictures that have been put on the Friends Graffiti Wall?** Read some of the responses on the wall and ask for comments about them. Have other words added as they are mentioned.

Friends often know things about each other that not everyone knows. We have an opportunity to find out some unusual things about the each other in this class. Distribute copies of the activity sheet "Autograph Bingo" (page 47). Explain that each person is to have the other students each autograph a square that has some information that describes him or her. If possible, limit the times one can sign the same card so everyone is included. As time allows, decide whether to have the students play until a row (vertical, horizontal, or diagonal) is filled with autographs or whether the entire card must be filled.

Your autograph cards describe some of the interesting things about people in this class. Getting to know each other is one of the important steps of a friendship. What are some other things you do to become a good friend? Allow for responses. **If these are qualities you like to have in your friends, how can you make sure you are also that kind of a friend?** Encourage discussion about the two-way responsibility of friendship, and the give and take that is required.

What about the friendships you are in right now? Do they show these

qualities or do you need to work on some of these areas?

Have you heard the phrase, "fair-weather friends"? What does it mean? (People who are around as long as things are pleasant and uncomplicated, but as soon as things start to get tough or require commitment and sacrifice they're out of your life.) **Fair-weather friends aren't real friends since they can't be counted on. They're not thinking about helping you to follow God's ways and be your best, but are selfish and self-centered with only their own pleasure and goals in mind. The things you wrote on the graffiti wall about what friends are *not* would describe fair-weather people.**

What are real friends like? (They keep confidences, pray and help when someone's hurt, cheer when others do well and choose wisely, take the initiative to call and check up on each other.) Real friends are different from fair–weather friends, since they are there for you, willing to listen, and stand up for you when you need it. **It's hard to accept sometimes, but it's the true friend who will say *no* when it's not a good idea, or push you to say *yes* when you are scared.**

What are the goals of good friendships? What happens to a friendship when each friend has a different goal for the friendship? (Friends know the value of being a friend. It takes time and effort to be the kind of friend others can count on.) **What are some of the hard things about being a friend?** (A friend uses positive pressure to help think through things and make wise decisions, help others follow God's way when they aren't sure they want to, to make a choice that's right even when your friend can't see it.)

Distribute copies of the activity sheet "Superstar Friends" (page 48). **Some Superstar Friends are described on your activity sheet. They can show you what an ideal friend is like.** Give students a chance to look over the descriptions of the Cheerleader, the Builder, the Jungle Guide, the Scientist, and the Pilot and Copilot and fill in some appropriate comments. The rest of the sheet is to be completed later.

Display the Unit Affirmation poster and read it all aloud together. Ask the students to think of a phrase to complete it. Choose one similar to "and be a caring, helpful friend." Write the selected phrase on the last line of the poster.

Let's look into the life of one true friend, a Hebrew young man, physically strong, well-informed, good-looking, and smart.

 Searching the Scripture (20 minutes)

This young friend was Daniel. The city Daniel lived in was invaded

by the Babylonian army and he and some of his friends were kidnapped. Explain to the class that the captors had deliberately stolen the finest young men in that city because they wanted to train them to serve their king, Nebuchadnezzar. Daniel and his friends were stolen from their families, schools, and synagogues, and taken to a different country. Three of Daniel's friends were Shadrach, Meshach, and Abednego.

Before these young men would serve their captor's king, they were to be given three years of in-depth educational training. They were to learn to speak and read a new language, and learn the ways of this new country. Since their captors didn't serve the true God, Daniel and his friends faced a lot of pressure to compromise their relationships to God and His Word. Part of their training included eating and drinking the food from the king's table. This sounds like an honor, but this food had been offered to idols and the Hebrew young men would be disobeying God's law if they ate it. Daniel faced a major choice and he also wanted to help his friends in this decision.

When you are in a situation with some potential pressure, you need to know why you are making the right decision. Daniel knew what the right decision would be, but he also wanted to convince his friends to do the right thing. Divide the class into two team to prepare for a debate between friends. Have one team represent Daniel's three friends, Shadrach, Meshach, and Abednego and argue against Daniel. Have the other team represent Daniel.

Ask the students to read Daniel 1:8-11 and plan how to present their side of the argument. Possible arguments for the three friends: We are visitors here, we shouldn't make them angry. Even the Official is afraid of the King. We don't want the responsibility of the Official losing his head because of us. Possible arguments for Daniel: God's standards are true for us even as prisoners. God will honor our faithfulness.

Have each team use its influence to persuade the other team of the dangers or justification for a choice. Then read verses 12-14 for the conclusion of the debate.

What do you think about this test? Do you think it could really work? How would you describe Daniel's attitude toward the guard? (Respectful and diplomatic.) Ask for a volunteer to read the result of the test in verses 15-17.

What were the results of the test and their obedience to God? (They passed the test and were given permission to continue obeying God's laws about their food.) God honored their trust in Him. He protected them and the Official from any harm from the king regarding the decision to not eat the

king's food. God also gave them help with the literature and learning in their training.

Three years have passed and the young prisoners are presented to the king for questioning. What might you do in their place? What was the result of their obedience to God and Daniel's influence on his friends? (They were the best; none was equal to them; they were ten times better than those who were now serving the king.) **Daniel wanted the best for his friends, and that included helping them follow God. His friendship and positive support helped all of them make the right decision in a difficult time.**

One way to be a good friend is to look at someone who already is one, and try to do some of the things they do, using them as a model. Have students complete the bottom portion of their activity sheet "Superstar Friends." **Daniel applied some of the Superstars' characteristics in his life and situation. Which ones do you see him modeling?** Have the students write the number of the appropriate cartoon character on the sheet. (The answers are: 1. builder; 2. scientist; 3. jungle guide.)

Read the Unit Verse together. Discuss what could be drawn or written on the heart of their Unit Verse Patterns. **When we are transformed by God's power we give Him not just our heart, but our friends and our actions. What guideline can we use that would show you have chosen to follow God's pattern?** Have the kids write a statement or two on their patterns, such as "I'll share what I know about Jesus as I share other things."

✔ Living the Lesson (5-10 minutes)

Before class, write each of these "As a Friend, I Would . . . ?" situations on separate 3" x 5" cards.

1. Rachel bought some glue for her art project, but her sister used it up without telling her. Dyanne knows Rachel is angry and encourages Rachel to . . . .

2. Paul's soccer team is having a victory celebration. Two of the guys plan to sneak some vodka into the punch. Paul doesn't want to have alcohol at the party, and he doesn't want his friends to get into trouble so . . . .

3. Maria became a Christian two weeks ago. Lydia knows Maria is a new Christian and is excited about following Jesus. One day Lydia notices Maria seems discouraged and decides to . . . .

4. Richard moved into the neighborhood two months ago and he isn't a Christian. Bob and Tyrone are on the church basketball team and have been praying for Richard. They come up with an idea and decide to . . . .

5. Ben and Jerry are in Adventure Club together at church. Ben thinks he caused his team to lose the relay when he fell while running. Ben mumbles that he's no good at anything and no one likes him. Jerry hears Ben and reminds Ben that . . . .

Form five groups and give each group one of the "As a Friend, I Would . . ." situation cards. Ask them to plan together how to roleplay this situation as a true friend.

Close this unit with prayer together, having the students pray a one sentence prayer of appreciation to God.

Autograph Bingo ✓

Find someone who fits a description and get an autograph. See how many DIFFERENT autographs you can collect.

good listener	has a nickname	been outside the USA	likes to talk	has been horse-back riding
likes video games	likes math	doesn't like video games	has a pet	enjoys science fiction books
good at helping others	talks to new people	**FREE SPACE**	has braces	knows how to rollerblade
has a freckle	likes to paint	has had stitches	has been outside the country	likes to eat mushrooms
doesn't like M&Ms	good at sports	likes to go shopping	has been to church camp	has done something nice for someone else today

Superstar Friends

God is helping you to be a superstar friend. Write something that you could say to one of your friends when he or she needs this kind of support.

WHAT WOULD YOU SAY?

1. **The Cheerleader:** an encourager who cheers when friends do wisely, has positive words to share, reaches out without waiting to be asked, cares when friends are down or hurt.

_____
_____
_____
_____

2. **The Builder:** one who knows God's way and sticks to it, doesn't compromise and helps friends to stand firm too.

_____
_____
_____
_____

3. **The Jungle Guide:** cuts the path through new territory and enables friends to come through it easier, is not afraid to stand up for what is right, knows how to witness to others.

_____
_____
_____
_____

4. **The Scientist:** the alternative finder, evaluating all the options for any given choice and helping friends choose what's best over what is merely okay.

_____
_____
_____
_____

5. **The Pilot and Copilot:** friends who work together by setting common goals, talking and sharing honestly and openly, and drawing on each others' strengths.

_____
_____
_____
_____

Daniel applied some of the Superstars' characteristics in his life and situation. Which ones do you see him modeling? Write the number of the Superstar on the line.

1. Daniel resolved to stick with the original plan from God and not compromise. (Daniel 1:8) _____

2. Daniel found an alternative and presents the plan. (Daniel 1:12, 13) _____

3. Daniel didn't seek just for himself, but cut the path for his friends too. (Daniel 1:12, 13) _____

Service Projects for Peer Pressure

In addition to the projects listed in these lessons, your class or church can also serve in the following ways:

✓ 1. Keep a class prayer journal about the needs of kids in your community or written about in the local newspaper. Write the need on the left side of the page and the answers to prayer on the right side. Use the class journal to help support each other through prayer and encouragement. It will also be a reminder of the ways God is at work in others' lives.

✓ 2. Perform the "Samson Rap" of Lesson Two for other groups, either in person, through video, or as a puppet play. Invite viewers of all ages to your class or present it at a church social function such as a pot-luck dinner.

✓ 3. Plan a way to begin a support group for other kids in your community. Publicize the group with flyers in public places such as stores, schools, and community bulletin boards.

✓ 4. Start a "United We Stand" newsletter or add a small section to the regular church bulletin. Give good news reports of kids overcoming pressures and being positive supports to each other. Feature articles of ways to succeed at applying the Unit Affirmation "I can learn to think for myself!"

Growing Includes Pain

No one can escape pain. Although it appears in different forms or measure, it comes to everyone. The question of this universal suffering may affect Christians harder because we believe an almighty powerful God rules the world and He lovingly plans the best for us.

Many in our culture deny death, yet the unwelcome reality is that suicide is one of the three leading causes of death among adolescents. In the last thirty years, adolescent suicide has tripled. Because a number of people now die in hospitals and other institutions without family nearby, many adults and children have never observed a death. These facts combine to produce a heightened fear of death. We fear what we don't understand.

Children cannot be sheltered forever from reality. If possible they need to be prepared to face pain and death before they encounter them. When we understand and can accept suffering, fear is changed to hope.

In this unit, you will have the opportunity to talk openly with your Juniors about these issues. Beginning with the universality of suffering you will discuss the truth that God is able to help us grow through painful experiences. By understanding the steps of grief we will be better equipped to support those who grieve. Talking about suicide in a loving, hopeful atmosphere will offer troubled kids an opportunity to ask for help. Throughout the unit your students will replace fear and helplessness with understanding and the glorious hope Christians have in God and His provisions for them.

 # Pain & Death Overview

Unit Verse: I consider that our present sufferings are not worth comparing with the glory that will be revealed in us. Romans 8:18

Unit Affirmation: I CAN GROW THROUGH PAINFUL EXPERIENCES!

LESSON	TITLE	OBJECTIVE	SCRIPTURE BASE
Lesson #1	Better or Bitter?	That your students will learn that suffering is universal and God is able to help us through painful experiences.	II Corinthians 11:23b-29; 12:7-10
Lesson #2	Good Grief	That your students will be able to understand the grieving process as well as support those around them who are grieving.	II Samuel 12:15-23
Lesson #3	Dead Loss	That your students will understand that because life is a gift from God our creator, it is precious and should be valued.	Numbers 11:10-17; I Kings 19:2-18
Lesson #4	Heavenly Daze	That your students will understand what God's Word teaches us about life after death.	I Corinthians 15:42-44; I Thessalonians 4:13-18

Partners

For the next few weeks your Junior-age child will be part of a group learning about Pain & Death. *Partners* is a planned parent piece to keep you informed of what will be taught during this exciting series.

PREVIEW...
Pain & Death

Everyone except God and His angels experiences pain and death. Yet these two subjects are often the last things we talk about with our children. Children's cancer, AIDS, and adolescent suicide are all on the increase. It is impossible to shield our kids from this reality.

In order to turn fear of the unknown into understanding and hope, your children need to be taught about pain and death before they encounter them. When suffering is imminent, personal feelings often get in the way and confuse any explanations we make to our kids. It is much wiser to talk about these painful topics when they seem distant and you can concentrate on truths, not feelings.

In the next few weeks, your kids will be learning about different aspects of pain and death. As they see God's enabling help and the values gained through pain they will be able to endure and overcome it. Because they will better understand and accept grief and death they will be freed to live. The basic point of what they will learn is summarized in the Unit Verse and the Unit Affirmation.

Unit Verse:

I consider that our present sufferings are not worth comparing with the glory that will be revealed in us. Romans 8:18

Unit Affirmation:

I CAN GROW THROUGH PAINFUL EXPERIENCES!

PRINCIPLES...
Pain & Death
PRINCIPLE #1:
PAIN IS UNIVERSAL AND GOD IS ABLE TO HELP US THROUGH IT.

Pain touches each one of us in some form. Through looking at the apostle Paul's experiences of suffering in II Corinthians 11:23b-29, and 12:7-10, your kids will see that God not only enables His children to endure pain, but they can rejoice in His overcoming strength.

PRINCIPLE #2:
GRIEVING PEOPLE WORK THROUGH A PROCESS OF GRIEF.

Professionals have identified emotional steps grieving people work through after loss. David's reaction to the death of his infant son in II Samuel 12:15-23, will help your kids see how these steps are expressed in life. They will be enabled to understand their own feelings of grief and support others who are grieving.

PRINCIPLE #3:
BECAUSE LIFE IS A GIFT FROM GOD, IT IS PRECIOUS AND WE SHOULD VALUE IT.

Suicide is one of the three leading causes of adolescent

deaths. Kids who resort to suicide see it as a last choice to escape unbearable pain. The stories of Moses in Numbers 11:10-17 and Elijah in I Kings 19:2-18 will show your kids the hope and help God offers severely depressed people.

PRINCIPLE #4:
GOD'S WORD TEACHES US ABOUT LIFE AFTER DEATH.

Many strange ideas about life after death are circulating throughout society today, including some Eastern religions and New Age teachings. When your kids understand what God's Word teaches about life after death in I Thessalonians 4:13-18 and I Corinthians 15:42-44, they will be better prepared to reject these false beliefs.

PRACTICE...

BUILDING A HEALTHY ATTITUDE TOWARD PAIN AND DEATH

You can reinforce what your child is learning in this unit by doing one or more of these at-home activities:

1. BIBLE ALIVE ACTIVITIES.

As a family, learn how to apply God's Word to situations involving pain and death.

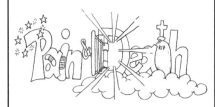

Become familiar with the psalms, such as Psalms 23, 46, and 91, which express our hope based on God's help. Study Scripture passages which teach the value of an individual life, such as Psalm 139. When you find stories of suffering in newspapers, magazines, or TV make it a practice to discuss how God can make a difference. Pray specifically for those who are suffering or grieving.

2. HIDE GOD'S WORD IN YOUR HEART.

As a family, memorize the Unit Verse. Then include Hebrews 2:14, 15 in your discussions. "By his death he might destroy him who holds the power of death—that is, the devil—and free those who all their lives were held in slavery by their fear of death." Use these verses as a constant reminder of God's help and hope for the suffering and grieving. Remember that when a Christian dies, other Christians are only separated from their friend for awhile!

3. KEEP COMMUNICATION

OPEN BETWEEN YOU AND YOUR CHILDREN.

Suicidal kids may have poor family or other relationships. Listen to your kid's feelings and don't make light of their fears or depression. Help them understand their feelings. Show you care. Honestly discuss their problems and assure them they always have choices other than suicide. Never lie to your children about death or try to sugarcoat its reality, but be careful not to go beyond their immediate area of interest or attention.

4. REACH OUT TO THE GRIEVING.

Lofty words or answers aren't necessary. Often the best thing you can do for grieving people is to simply be with them. Crying with them, allowing them to talk about their loss, and hugging are helpful responses and easy to do. Tokens of sympathy and love such as cards, food, and prayers are also supportive. The hardest time for grieving people is about two weeks after a funeral when everyone has gone home and they face life on their own. Our Christian support is essential. Time does help heal the wounds of grief, but God's love flowing out of His children can prevent scar tissue from forming.

Lesson 1

Better or Bitter?

Aim: That your students will learn that suffering is universal and God is able to help us through painful experiences.

Scripture: II Corinthians 11:23b-29; 12:7-10

Unit Verse: I consider that our present sufferings are not worth comparing with the glory that will be revealed in us. Romans 8:18

Unit Affirmation: I CAN GROW THROUGH PAINFUL EXPERIENCES!

 Planning Ahead

1. Photocopy Activity Sheets (pages 59 and 60)—one for each student.
2. Prepare the Unit Affirmation poster by writing across the top of a large poster board the words: I CAN GROW THROUGH PAINFUL EXPERIENCES! Under the title, write the numbers 1-4 vertically down the left-hand side.
3. Prepare the Instructions poster for making "What to do" booklets. Write the following on a large piece of paper or poster board:
   > Welcome! Let's get started today by making a booklet for our Unit Verse.
   > A. Fold two pieces of paper in half and put them together like a book.
   > B. Write "What to Do When it Hurts" on the cover.
   > C. Copy this Unit Verse on the top of the first page: "I consider that our present sufferings are not worth comparing with the glory that will be revealed in us." Romans 8:18.
4. **OPTIONAL:** Prepare two identical cups of water. Fill one cup with clean water. Fill the second cup with water and add a little dirt. Both cups should be brimful.

1 Setting the Stage (5-10 minutes)

WHAT YOU'LL DO
- Make "What to Do" booklet covers

WHAT YOU'LL NEED
- Instructions poster
- Colored markers or pens
- **OPTIONAL:** Sample booklet

2 Introducing the Issue (20 minutes)

WHAT YOU'LL DO
- Use an activity sheet to discuss different kinds of suffering
- Introduce the Unit Affirmation poster

WHAT YOU'LL NEED
- "A World of Possibilities" Activity Sheet (page 59)
- Unit Affirmation poster

3 Searching the Scriptures (20 minutes)

WHAT YOU'LL DO
- Complete an imaginary resumé to learn about Paul's painful experiences
- Write a statement to illustrate how to view painful experiences

WHAT YOU'LL NEED
- "Pain Yields Gain" Activity Sheet (page 60)
- **OPTIONAL:** Two cups of water, newspaper or paper towels
- Students' "What to Do" booklets

4 Living the Lesson (5-10 minutes)

WHAT YOU'LL DO
- List ways God helps us when we suffer
- Use a "handwritten" pledge to express trust in God's willingness and ability to help

WHAT YOU'LL NEED
- Watercolor markers

 *Lesson 1*

 # Setting the Stage (5-10 minutes)

Display the Instruction poster and have students make a "What to Do" booklet as they arrive today. As they do this, focus their attention on feelings involved in suffering. Point out similarities and differences between their experiences of suffering. **How many of you have been sick? How many suffered a broken friendship? Have you had a pet that got sick and died? Have you felt lonely or thought no one understood the pain you were feeling? Do you feel badly about the problems of pollution or endangered species?** When everyone is finished, put aside the booklets to be used later in this lesson and introduce the topic for this unit. **For the next few weeks we are going to talk about pain and death. We're going to learn to identify pain, how to respond to it, and how to help others who are suffering.**

 # Introducing the Issue (20 minutes)

Here's an imagination starter. Distribute the activity sheet "A World of Possibilities" (page 59). Ask a volunteer to read the opening paragraph. Kids will have an opportunity to design a perfect world. Let them spend about five–seven minutes on this activity. Invite students to share their designs with the group.

When God created the world He made it perfect. Have a student read Genesis 1:31. **How did God feel about His world?** (Everything was very good.) **Do the "perfect" worlds you designed and the one God originally created differ from the one we live in now? If so, how?** (Now there are bad things like pain, war, pollution, sickness, death.) **When sin entered the world, so did these things. God made a beautiful showplace when He created the world, but this good, perfect place became distorted by sin and Satan.**

How many of you have never had some kind of pain in your life? (No one.) The truth is that no one can escape pain. It might come as physical pain, broken relationships, pollution of nature, or the knowledge of a troublesome personal sin which causes God and you grief. **Name some pains you have suffered.** Allow students to respond. Their answers might include: broken friendship; physical or mental disability; parent's divorce; death of a favorite pet, loved family member or friend. Consider sharing a personal pain you have

felt. Depending on how comfortable your students are about sharing you might choose to have kids write down their pains on slips of paper. Have them fold these over so no one else can see them. Collect the slips and read them as anonymous contributions to the discussion.

Make your classroom a safe place for kids to feel secure enough to share the personal hurts and fears they have. Listen to their problems with an open mind and compassionate heart. Don't act shocked by anything students confess or discuss. Also be sensitive to the way the students react to each other. Be careful to stress the personal nature of these lessons. You may see the necessity of offering to talk to a student privately away from the group. You may be the only one they feel comfortable enough with to tell these things. Just being there with your kids in their pain is very supportive to them. The two most helpful comments you can make are, "Thank you for sharing your pain with me," and "I hurt with you."

The problem of pain may be harder for Christians than nonbelievers because we believe God is all-powerful, loves us, and wants the best for us. **If you could ask God to answer one question about pain, what would it be?** Encourage students to honestly share their fears and doubts about suffering. God wants us to trust Him with our honest questioning. Job, Paul, and even Jesus expressed their anguish to God. Some common questions are "Why does God allow pain?" "If God wants the best for me, why doesn't He heal this sickness?"

While no one has all the answers to these questions, we can be assured that God is still in charge. God turns even the worst suffering into blessings for His children. We may not recognize the good of it until we are in heaven, but God does want what is best for each of us. God's plan for His children is infinitely greater than to merely make us happy. If happiness depends on our surroundings or situations, then it changes as they change. God's goal is for His children to become like His Son, Jesus Christ, in every way. To reach that goal He often uses the transforming power of pain.

Display the Unit Affirmation poster. Read it aloud together. Ask students to think of a phrase they can add to the first line that describes one thing they learned today that will help them grow through painful experiences. Choose one that says something like, "by trusting God to turn bad things into good, even when I can't see the good." Write this phrase on the first line.

Let's find out how one faithful follower of God felt about the pain he experienced.

✔ Searching the Scriptures (20 minutes)

Distribute the activity sheet "Pain Yields Gain" (page 60). Ask someone to read the directions aloud. Students can work together in pairs to complete this activity.

What pains did Paul undergo? (Prison; beatings; shipwrecks; danger of drowning, robbery, betrayal; sleep deprivation; hunger and thirst; cold; mental worries about all the churches; physical disability.) Point out this includes all the different areas of pain: physical, mental, emotional, and spiritual. **What does this tell us about the difference in pain experiences between followers of Jesus and non-followers?** (No difference; both suffer the same kinds of pain.) **Pain and suffering come to the lives of everyone who lives on this planet. Christians are not spared from suffering. Pain is not imaginary. It is real and hurts!**

Even though God allows pain to come to us we can also trust Him to bring good out of it. Most pain in our lives happens just because we are human beings. Often pain is the way that we gain the greatest knowledge and fellowship with Jesus. When people think back on the hard times in their lives they realize those are the times they were closest to God. Times of suffering help us put things in focus. They force us to reconsider what is important in life. Pain also makes us concentrate on the things in our lives that keep us from loving and serving God wholeheartedly.

What does the Bible say Paul did about the "thorn in the flesh" that he suffered? (Pleaded three times with the Lord to remove it.) **We need to be honest about our feelings in times of suffering. It's OK to cry for ourselves and others. We should remove pain if at all possible, but realize that although God sees everything, we may not always understand why He doesn't remove the pain. That's when we learn to trust in God's best for us anyway. Fear that the suffering will never end can push a painful experience into the area of the unbearable. Helplessness can also lead to despair and bitterness.**

A suffering person must have hope in order to survive pain. Paul placed his hope in God. He believed that God could bring good results from his suffering. Because of Jesus' victory over sin by His death on the cross, pain can be transformed into victory. Have students check out Romans 5:3-5 to see what values trusting in God can produce in suffering followers. (Perseverance, character, hope, and love.)

OPTIONAL: Display the two cups of water. These cups should be so full that they will spill over when you bump them. Put newspaper or paper towels under them. Gather the group around you so they can easily see but not so close they will get splattered. The cup with clear water represents the life of a follower of Jesus. The cup with the dirty water illustrates a life without Him.

Bump the cups so water spills out. When pain strikes people whatever is in them spills out. If they are filled with fear and helplessness, bitterness spills out. If the power of God is in them, trust in His enabling help will be seen by everyone around them. Pain clearly points to the life of Jesus in a follower.

If Paul had never suffered what do you think the people he worked with would have thought of him? (Special, different, so holy and perfect they could never identify with him.) **How do you think they felt about him when they saw he experienced pain just as they did?** (More friendly, one of them, a human being who also needed love and comfort.) **Paul was an example to everyone of the Lord's power because he not only endured pain, but trusted God would enable him to overcome it and change him for the better because of it.**

How does II Corinthians 12:10 compare with what seems obvious about strength and weakness? (Just the opposite, you have to be strong to be powerful.) **What do you think God meant when He said His power can be made perfect in weakness?** Let kids look up II Corinthians 4:6, 7 for a clue. **When we are weak, people can see that any power we have is from God. God doesn't always rescue us or make suffering easier, but proves He can help us endure and overcome it.**

Have students use the "What to Do" booklets they made and read the Unit Verse together. Emphasize that all our pains are temporary. Christians expectantly await a world where every tear will be wiped away and suffering will disappear. Paul was so convinced of this he staked his work, health, and life on God's promises. Joy in the midst of suffering comes not from the pain, but because of trust in our all-powerful God.

Let the group suggest a thought that illustrates this. You might use one like, "Because God is willing to help us, we can be winners through painful experiences." Have the students write the sentence on the first page of their booklets. Then keep the booklets together to be used in the next weeks' lessons.

☑ Living the Lesson (5-10 minutes)

Christian doctors and counselors have noticed that people get bitter if they focus on questions about why they suffer or who is responsible for their pain. People who got better concentrated on their response to trust God fully despite their painful condition.

Our attitude makes a difference. When we trust God in our pain it leaves us with a solid faith in Him that no amount of suffering can destroy. Have students turn to Psalm 50:15 and read it aloud together. **God is willing and able to help you when you suffer. Jesus has shared pain with us because He has also hurt, cried, and suffered. He can sympathize with us.**

What are some ways God can help us when we suffer? List these on the board or a large piece of paper. Examples: He can give us His supernatural strength for our spirits and emotions, medicine, doctors, prayers of others for us, strengthened faith in God, friendship of family of God, deeper knowledge of and trust in God, hope of wonderful new world where pain will be no more.

Briefly review ways God can help your students when they suffer. Have each person write some of these on one of his or her hands with watercolor markers. Close with a silent prayer and this challenging "handwritten" pledge: **If you trust God to help you when you suffer, raise the hand you wrote on and pledge your faith to God. Thank Him for His help in sorrow and tell Him you trust in Him.**

A World of Possibilities

If you could design a perfect world, what would it be like? Think about the people, animals, plants, and environment. Use pictures or words to describe this perfect world. How would all these things get along with each other?

Things I would put in my perfect world:

_____

_____

_____

_____

_____

_____

Things I would leave out of my perfect world:

_____

_____

_____

_____

_____

_____

_____

Relationship between people, animals, plants, environment:

_____

_____

_____

_____

_____

_____

_____

Pain Yields Gain

You are Paul's secretary helping him complete a resumé describing his work experience and qualifications. Read each reference and then complete the form using information from the Scriptures. Write the data on the line beside each section.

Company: Family of God
Employer: God Almighty
Job Opening: Follower of Jesus, first-class

Name of Applicant: Paul of Tarsus
Positions Held: _____

_____

Past: Trainee, pain program
Present: Apostle, Missionary

Work Experience:

I Corinthians 11:23b-27 _____

_____

Special Interests:

II Corinthians 11:28, 29 _____

_____

Personal Remarks:

II Corinthians 12:7, 8 _____

_____

Comments about training program:

II Corinthians 12:9, 10

_____

_____

Romans 5:3-5

Suffering produces _____, which in turn produces

_____, which then gives us _____, which

comes from _____ love poured into our hearts.

Lesson 2

Good Grief

Aim: That your students will be able to understand the grieving process as well as support those around them who are grieving.

Scripture: II Samuel 12:15-23

Unit Verse: I consider that our present sufferings are not worth comparing with the glory that will be revealed in us. Romans 8:18

Unit Affirmation: I CAN GROW THROUGH PAINFUL EXPERIENCES!

 Planning Ahead

1. Photocopy Activity Sheets (pages 68 and 69)—one for each student.
2. Prepare cue cards by cutting 3" x 5" cards in half, making two cards from each. Write one of the following words on each card: shock, denial, guilt, anger, resentment, fear, depression, hopelessness, acceptance. If necessary, add several other words describing emotions or have duplicates of the above words so each student has a card.

 Setting the Stage (5-10 minutes)

WHAT YOU'LL DO

- Participate in a game to become sensitive to emotions involved in the grieving process

WHAT YOU'LL NEED

- Cue cards

 Introducing the Issue (20 minutes)

WHAT YOU'LL DO

- Use an activity sheet to identify the steps of grief
- Act out appropriate and inappropriate things to say or do with a grieving friend
- Add a phrase to the Unit Affirmation poster

WHAT YOU'LL NEED

- "Growing Through Grief" Activity Sheet (page 67)
- Unit Affirmation poster

Searching the Scriptures (20 minutes)

WHAT YOU'LL DO

- Discover how a loving father grieved when his child died
- Write a statement about trust

WHAT YOU'LL NEED

- "A Father's Viewpoint" Activity Sheet (page 68)
- Unit Verse "What to Do" booklets

 Living the Lesson (5-10 minutes)

WHAT YOU'LL DO

- Recognize ways God can help us cope with grief

WHAT YOU'LL NEED

- List of ways to share comfort

 *Lesson 2*

 # Setting the Stage (5-10 minutes)

As students arrive have them draw a cue card to pantomime. They are to keep secret the emotion described on their card. Players takes turns acting out the emotion on their cards while the group tries to guess the answer. Stop play after three—five minutes.

Was it easy to guess the feelings in this game? Why? (No, people express their feelings in different ways; Yes, our faces and body language tell a lot about what we are feeling.) **Because people show their emotions in different ways it is sometimes hard to understand what they are really feeling.** Discuss one emotion, such as anger, as an example. People usually show this by changes in facial color, clenching fists, shouting, or getting excited. However, some individuals may resort to silence and stop eating instead. **Our suffering is much more complex than what is seen on the surface. Sometimes we don't even understand ourselves.**

Many of the feelings you pantomimed are involved in grief or loss. Although we usually associate grief with death, it can come about because of a loss of any kind. What are some things we grieve about? (Someone dying, a pet's death, loss of a friend, loss of a goal or hope (example: athlete has injury which ends career), parents' divorce, personal sickness, drug addiction.) **What does it feel like to lose something so important to you?** (Scary; I might die too; I don't know.) **What do you think people do when a loss like this occurs?** (Cry, accept it and go on, get angry, act like it doesn't bother them.) **When people are grieving they go through a process that involves several different steps. Today we're going to look at these steps and talk about how we can help ourselves and others.**

 # Introducing the Issue (20 minutes)

Distribute copies of the activity sheet "Growing Through Grief" (page 67). Ask someone to read the directions aloud. Have the students work in groups of two or three to complete this activity.

The activity sheet shows the stages in the grieving process. I'll list them so everyone can see them. On a chalkboard or large sheet of paper write the numbers one through five vertically on the left side. Write the words DENIAL, ANGER, BARGAINING, DEPRESSION, and ACCEPTANCE beside the numbers. **Let's take a look at each of these.**

Denial is when a person is shocked by the loss and can't believe it is true. The person thinks "It happens to other people—not to me!" Find

an example on the activity sheet. (Kids don't die!) **What are some other kinds of suffering that can cause that feeling?** Young people tend to think they are immortal. When warned about dangers such as cancer, drugs, AIDS, or reckless actions that jeopardize life, they think those things only happen to older people or someone else.

Anger or resentment is usually the next stage of grieving. Can you identify which statement represents this? (God, I hate You . . .) **Grieving persons get angry at the people they think are responsible for making the loss happen. They are feeling such emotional pain that sometimes they are angry at doctors or God or even the person who died. This is a normal stage of grief. When people are in this stage it is easy to think they have lost their faith in God. This isn't true. They need to express their frustration and work through this part of the grieving process.**

Bargaining is often the next part of the grief process. The person tries to talk God into doing something else in exchange for something to escape or change the loss. Which quote shows this? (If You . . . I'll . . .) Some losses are caused by our own bad choices. (Example: being careless with a skateboard). The majority of loss is brought on by situations over which we have no control, so bargaining can't affect the loss.

Another stage of grieving is depression. This is a hopeless feeling that there is no purpose to anything. What is the example of this? (Why do...can't do anything!) This is a dangerous stage for young people because they tend to feel things so powerfully. They believe the emotion of the moment will last forever. Acting on depression leads to suicide for many kids. Depression is a paralyzing feeling because it prevents us from doing things. When we realize other people have had the same experiences and overcome the loss, we are led on into the final step of grief. Point out Christians such as Joni Eareckson Tada and Dave Dravecky of the San Francisco Giants who overcame tremendous physical losses and became role models.

The last stage of grief is acceptance. This is the "making peace" with God step. Which situation fits this step? (I miss . . . but I know . . .) We accept the truth that we can't change the loss, but are thankful for having had the person, goal, or relationship and now readjust our lives to go on.

Write the numbers six and seven on your list. There are also two other steps that many young people experience in their grief. Beside these numbers write GUILT and FEAR. Kids often feel guilty about somehow causing the loss to someone else. Because they don't understand the causes behind losses, kids feel somehow responsible for them. Divorce is one example. Many times kids are afraid that what happened to someone close to them will also happen to them. As above, what we don't understand we fear.

Ask for several volunteers to choose a partner and act out the responses they wrote on the bottom half of the activity sheet. Then discuss their ideas.

Display the Unit Affirmation poster. Ask the group to read it aloud together. **When we recognize and understand the grieving process we don't need to worry that a person has stopped trusting in God. We will realize they are normal and just working through their sorrow.** Have students suggest phrases to add to the poster. Select one similar to "when I understand how grieving people feel." Write this on the second line.

Not everyone experiences all these steps or goes through them in the order we discussed. Turn to II Samuel 12:15-23 and we'll see how a loving father grieved over the death of his child.

 # Searching the Scriptures (20 minutes)

Distribute copies of the activity sheet "A Father's Viewpoint" (page 68). This is an imaginary diary (although the story is true) that King David might have written when his son died. Have students take turns reading the diary entries aloud. **Based on the diary, how do you think David felt about his child?** (Loved him, wanted to take good care of him, sad because he was sick.)

Refer to the list of stages in the grief process. **As we talk about the entries in David's diary, see if you can help me identify the steps he went through. We'll check them off as we do.**

What is the first grief stage you find? (Guilt.) David felt he was to blame for his baby's illness. He was sorry for his sin and God restored the broken relationship between them, but David still thought it was his fault.

What did David ask God to do? (Spare the baby's life.) **In the next diary entry, how did David feel about God?** (Angry.) Although not mentioned in Scripture, David might have experienced this feeling coupled with guilt knowing he was the one who should have died.

Look at the third entry in David's diary. What stage of grief do you think it describes? (Bargaining.) This is an "If You will . . . Then I will" thing. **What did David want God to do?** (Let the baby live.) **In return, what did he do?** (Went without food and spent all his time praying.)

Ask a volunteer to read II Samuel 15:17. **How did David's friends react to his behavior?** (Urged him to eat with them and get up from the ground.) **When we don't understand what a grieving person is suffering, sometimes we try to prove they are wrong. Often the best thing we can do is listen to them or show them our support by just being with them. If David's friends had tried that, what might they have done to comfort him?** (Prayed with him, sat with him, offered to go without food.)

What stage of grief does the next diary entry picture? (Depression or hopelessness.) **How did David feel about God during this stage of grief?** (God was far away, wasn't listening to his prayers.) **Why do you think he might have felt like this?** (Things had gotten worse, thought the baby would die.) **The times when God is silent are often the hardest times of all. We have to hold on by faith and believe that what His Word says is true without actually seeing it fulfilled.**

A loss of any kind brings an ending to things as they were, such as a planned goal, a relationship, or personal self-esteem. The grieving person realizes that something is over—the loss is final. If people don't have someone they can turn to for emotional support, the depression can be devastating to the point where the grieving person considers suicide to end the pain.

What grief step is found in the last entry? (Acceptance.) This is when people face their loss calmly. Read II Samuel 15:20. **What did David do when he reached this stage?** (Got up, washed, put on lotions, changed clothes, went to God's house and worshiped Him.) **In the diary, David thanked God for several things. What were they?** (Gift of the baby, allowing him to love and take care of him, promise of eternal life.)

David accepted God's will. He had grown through his painful experience. David's grief helped him to acknowledge God as the giver of all life. It taught him what was really important in life. Through it he had a deeper relationship with God which then flowed out through the psalms he wrote to bless and comfort us.

Ask students to turn to Romans 8:18 and read it aloud together. **What do you think David would have thought about this verse?** (Agreed with it.) Second Samuel 12:23 is how David might have written our Unit Verse. **What glory was revealed in David's life because of his grief?** (The promise of going to be with his child.) **David's hope of being with his child in heaven comforted him in his grief.**

Have the group suggest a go-along statement on grief to add to their Unit Verse "What to Do" booklets. Choose something like, "When we are grieving, we can trust God's promises." Let them write this on the second page. Hope in God and His promises is a big comfort in times of grief.

✔ Living the Lesson (5-10 minutes)

A well-known Christian author wrote, "Time heals grief. Love prevents scar tissue from forming." He was talking about the love of God and also the love of other people. How does God show His love to us by helping us handle grief? Mention tangible ways: friends who send cards,

call, or bring food; the church family who prays for us; doctors, nurses, health workers, and hospitals to ease our pain; counselors and pastors to help us understand what we are feeling. Also talk about intangible ways: God's gifts of strength to go on; hope; courage; the promises of eternal life and a heavenly home which Jesus Christ obtained for His followers by His death and resurrection. **God is always with us in our troubles and is ready to help us through them.**

Ask the group to turn to II Corinthians 1:4 and read it silently. **What is one advantage we receive from troubles?** (We can comfort others with the same comfort God gives us.) **When people are grieving they find that people who really understand their pain are those who have had the same experiences.**

Have someone read aloud Psalm 9:9-12, 18. In many translations musical directions on this psalm say "To the tune of 'The Death of the Son.' " Whether or not this is directly tied to the child he lost, David's psalm shows the faithfulness of God to those who are grieving. David's pain and grief are expressed through the psalms he wrote. **When you have an opportunity to offer support to others who are grieving, remember God's help to you and share it with them.**

Close with a prayer of thanksgiving for God's love and comfort in times of grief.

Growing Through Grief

What do people say when they are hurting and in pain? What is the Bible's response? Read what some kids have said or thought. Then look up the Scripture reference and fill in what the Bible says.

"My little sister can't be dead. Kids don't die."
Ecclesiastes 7:2b Death is the _____ of every_____.

"I was jealous of my sister. That's why she has cancer."
Psalm 103:10, 11 God does not pay us back according to our _____.

"I'm afraid I'll get sick and die like my brother."
Isaiah 41:10 Do not _____. I (God) am with _____.

" God, I hate You because You let my Dad die."
Romans 5:12 Death comes to all _____, because of _____.

"If You stop my parents' divorce, I'll be a pastor."
Matthew 26:39 Even Jesus said, "Not my _____, but God's _____"

"Why do exercises? One-legged people can't do anything!"
Philippians 1:20 I need sufficient _____, so that _____will be exalted in every-thing I do.

"I miss Grandpa, but I know he's happy in heaven."
II Corinthians 1:4 God _____ us in our troubles, so we may _____ others.

CHOOSE one of the above situations. You are a good friend of the person who said that. Write down one thing you can say to your friend that would be helpful. Write down one thing NOT to say.

A HELPFUL THING TO SAY | SOMETHING NOT TO SAY

_____   _____

_____   _____

_____   _____

A Father's Viewpoint

Dear Diary,

Our baby boy has become very ill. If I had not sinned against the Lord this would never have happened! I am praying that God will make my son well again.

Dear Diary,

My child is getting worse. I feel so helpless. If only there were something I could do for him. Why won't God answer my prayers? It's not fair that a baby should die without ever having enjoyed life!

Dear Diary,

I have decided to go without food and spend my days and nights earnestly praying to God. Maybe this will show the Lord I'm really sorry and He won't let the baby die. My friends and family have been trying to comfort me about my son. They want me to eat and live a normal life, but they just don't understand how I feel. How can life be normal when my child gets worse every day?

Dear Diary,

I am really sad. Instead of getting better, our baby is worse. It looks like he is going to die. I feel that God is far away. My prayers seem worthless. My heart aches and I've cried until there are no tears left.

Dear Diary,

Seven days have gone by since my son got sick. Today I noticed that my servants were whispering together. I realized that my little boy was dead. I got up, washed, and changed clothes. Then I went to the temple to worship the Lord.

I thanked God for the gift of my baby son and the brief time I had to love and care for him. The baby is now safe in the arms of his loving, heavenly Father. I can never bring him back to me, but someday God will take me to be with him forever. Praise God for His wonderful promise of eternal life where there won't be any tears, pain, or suffering! Until then, I will serve the Lord and try my best to follow and honor Him every day.

Lesson 3

Dead Loss

Aim: That your students will understand that because life is a gift from God our creator, it is precious and should be valued.

Scripture: Numbers 11:10-17; I Kings 19:2-18

Unit Verse: I consider that our present sufferings are not worth comparing with the glory that will be revealed in us. Romans 8:18

Unit Affirmation: I CAN GROW THROUGH PAINFUL EXPERIENCES!

 Planning Ahead

1. Photocopy Activity Sheets (pages 75 and 76)—one for each student.
2. Write each of the following Warning Signs on separate pieces of paper, using a variety of colors of paper. "1. a preoccupation about death, such as wondering how it would feel to be dead" "2. changes in personality or mood" "3. changes in eating or sleeping" "4. withdrawing from friends and activities" "5. takes risks that show they have little value for life" "6. abuses drugs" "7. gives away prized possessions to friends" "8. tells you they are thinking about ending life" " 9. tells you not to tell anyone"
3. Make nine Get Help signs, on identical color and size paper (about 8 1/2 x 11). Write the words "Get Help from a Trusted Adult" on each one.
4. Prepare a Resource Information handout by listing local agencies such as your church, youth center, police department, hospital emergency room, mental health clinic, family service organization, crisis hotline center. Include the National Teen Suicide Hotline number, 800-621-4000 which gives information and help 24 hours a day.
5. **OPTIONAL:** Call your local school district and ask for suicide prevention educational materials that are available. This will also help you know what is accessible in your area.

1 Setting the Stage (5-10 minutes)

WHAT YOU'LL DO

- Participate in a stunt to experience the feeling of hopelessness

WHAT YOU'LL NEED

- Pennies—enough for half the number of students

2 Introducing the Issue (20 minutes)

WHAT YOU'LL DO

- Use an activity sheet to define reasons people choose to end life
- Create a clothesline of possible warning signs and how to help
- Add a phrase to the Unit Affirmation poster

WHAT YOU'LL NEED

- "Dying to Know" Activity Sheet (page 75)
- Warning Signs and Get Help Signs
- Heavy yarn or twine at least 12 feet long
- Nine clothespins, stapler
- Unit Affirmation poster

3 Searching the Scriptures (20 minutes)

WHAT YOU'LL DO

- Participate in an imaginary guest show to discuss God's comfort
- Write a statement about enduring suffering

WHAT YOU'LL NEED

- "The Sighs That Bind" Activity Sheet (page 76)
- Unit Verse "What to Do" booklets

4 Living the Lesson (5-10 minutes)

WHAT YOU'LL DO

- Discuss ways to be helpful to others who need comfort resources

WHAT YOU'LL NEED

- Resource Information handouts

Setting the Stage (5-10 minutes)

As students arrive, have them find a partner and give each pair a penny. Have one partner put fingers of one hand touching the tips of the fingers on the other hand. The other partner places a penny between the tips of the ring fingers. The object of the stunt is to open the ring fingers and drop the penny. They should be able to accomplish this task rather easily.

Now have the pairs try the trick again but this time they must keep the tips of the ring fingers together and fold the rest of the fingers down so the knuckles are touching. Players are not allowed to slide fingers apart! This time they are unable to drop the coin.

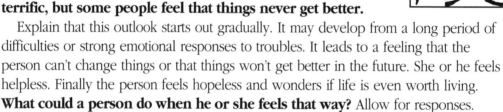

How did you feel when you tried the trick the first time? (Happy, proud, satisfied.) **How did you feel the second time?** (Discouraged, upset, hopeless.) **Most of us have discouraging times when everything seems to go wrong. Of course, this was just a short trick to give you an example of feelings. For most of us, frustrating times are balanced with times when life is terrific, but some people feel that things never get better.**

Explain that this outlook starts out gradually. It may develop from a long period of difficulties or strong emotional responses to troubles. It leads to a feeling that the person can't change things or that things won't get better in the future. She or he feels helpless. Finally the person feels hopeless and wonders if life is even worth living. **What could a person do when he or she feels that way?** Allow for responses.

Introducing the Issue (20 minutes)

Imagine one day you saw me cutting my arm off. You would be upset and ask me why I was doing such a terrible thing. I say, "Because I have a sliver in my finger and I can't stand the pain anymore." What would you think? (That's a crazy reason, a stupid way to solve the problem.) **As foolish as this imaginary situation seems, it is similar to the way some people try to solve their troubles. Let's find out something about these people and why they might choose to end their pain in this inappropriate way.**

What causes a person to die? (Usually illness, something wrong with their physical body, or an accident.) **Would a person choose to die?** (Usually not, unless they were so discouraged and thought their problems would never get better.) **Have you heard the word "suicide?" What does it mean? What do you know about suicide?** Take the time to listen carefully to the students' explanation. This may be a subject that has not been openly talked about and they may have misconceptions and fears that need to be discussed and clarified.

Distribute copies of the activity sheet "Dying to Know" (page 75). Have students spend a few minutes working on this individually or in small groups. Discuss the answers together, using the following information. Answers are: false, true, false, true, false, true.

People who turn to suicide are normal people. They have good days and bad days. Then things change. Every day seems like a bad one without any hope of ever getting better. They may not know how to find help and think suicide is the only choice they have left.

Anyone who thinks the pain is never-ending may be tempted to think about suicide as the only way to stop their suffering. They feel hollow inside and eventually lose hope. When they have no hope they see no possibility of an end to their pain other than by death.

Any threats of suicide need to be taken seriously. When people talk about taking their lives they are really informing you they are desperate and are pleading for help.

People who are thinking about ending their lives usually give several warning signs. Ask for two volunteers to become clothesline poles and hold the ends of the yarn or twine about three feet from the floor. If it is possible, you may want to attach the clothesline to the wall. Distribute the first seven Warning Signs to students and have them use a clothespin to attach each sign to the line. Read the first Warning Sign. **What can you do if someone you know seems to always think, read, or talk about death and dying? Should you just ignore it?** Give a student one of the Get Help signs and have it stapled or taped to the warning sign. Continue discussing the warning signs and have a different student attach a Get Help sign to each one.

Talking to severely depressed people offers them a chance to ask for help. Talking opens a channel for them to express their feelings. Listen carefully to what they say and don't downplay their feelings. You don't need to have a lot of ready answers for them. The main thing is to express how much you care for them and value their friendship.

How would you feel if your friend told you he or she was thinking about ending his or her life? (Terrible, afraid, worried.) Have someone attach #8 Warning Sign "tells you they're thinking about ending life" to the line. **What do you do?** Everyone says together "Get Help." Attach a "Get Help" sign.

Suppose your friend asks you to promise not to tell anyone about his or her feelings? What do you think you should do? (Not break your promise, refuse to promise, tell anyway.) Put up the last sign "tells you not to tell anyone." **This is really a matter of life and death. If you share this with other trusted people you are able to help your friend.** Ask someone to attach the "Get Help" sign. **How do you think your friend might feel if you told someone else so they could help?** (Angry, mad enough to not be your friend anymore.) Some choices are difficult to make, but remind your students that a person's life is at stake here. It's better to tell and have an angry, live friend than to keep the secret and have a

dead friend! Look at the clothesline. **Is there ever a time you should not get help from a trusted adult?**

Feelings that have pushed people to attempt to take their lives are only temporary, but these people don't realize that. When people are offered hope and begin to find good ways to handle their problems they are ready to face life again. It is important to treat these people the same as everyone else when they get back into normal life again. No one wants to be treated like an outcast.

Display the Unit Affirmation poster. Read it aloud together. **Everyone has times when everything seems to go wrong and we look for an escape from our pain. God can give us true and honest hope for the future and help us get through these discouraging times. What phrase can we add to the next line of our poster?** Have the group offer ideas. You might choose one like "by accepting the hope God gives us, and asking someone in His family for help" or "by thanking God for the gift of life." Write the phrase on the third line.

Even some of the giants of faith in the Bible had times when they thought nobody cared about or understood them. They thought life wasn't worth living. We're going to listen to an imaginary TV talk show today and see how two of these people felt and what kind of help they found.

Searching the Scriptures (20 minutes)

Distribute copies of the activity sheet "The Sighs That Bind" (page 76). You will need three people to take the parts of Kid Toppel, Moses, and Elijah. Have them sit together in one area of the room as though they were a Host and two Guests. Get everyone involved by having remaining students be newspaper reporters that take notes. They can mark important parts of the skit for later discussion.

According to the skit what great things had Moses and Elijah just experienced? (Moses led the Israelites across the Red Sea and Elijah defeated the Baal prophets and ended a three-year drought.) Have the reporters respond as you do through this discussion.

In the drama both men thought people were not treating them right. Why did they think this? (They never thanked them, complained all the time, didn't stand up for them when they were in trouble.) **How do you think this made them feel?** (Lonely, afraid, angry, hopeless.) **These great leaders of God were just like people today. They thought nobody knew or understood how they felt. They believed that people didn't care. Others were too involved with their own problems to think about the troubles Moses and Elijah had.**

Do you ever feel depressed? If so, why? Make your class a warm, caring place where kids feel safe to share their feelings and problems. One of the reasons kids

this age get depressed easily is because they are beginning to change in so many ways—physically, emotionally, and even spiritually. Many of their emotions seem exaggerated at this stage. They may feel like they're on a roller coaster of feelings. It's hard for them to realize their feelings are usually only temporary.

What did the skit say Moses and Elijah did when they felt life was meaningless? (Ran away, talked to God about it, asked God to end their lives.) **What do you do when you feel really down?** Let students respond. Some of the most common ways kids cope are by listening to music, watching TV, and daydreaming. Encourage them to know that it's OK to have feelings, even depressing ones. Feelings are neither right nor wrong. It's what we do about them that makes the difference. Ask someone to look up John 10:10b and read it aloud. **Who can make our lives worthwhile?** (Jesus.)

Have students look up Numbers 11:16, 17. **How did God help Moses?** (Gave him seventy helpers who also wanted to honor God.) **How do you think that comforted him?** (He wouldn't feel alone anymore, could share the problems with them.) When we get burdened down by too many duties or too hard a task it's easy to become tired out and discouraged. Kids often get involved in too many activities and feel stressed-out and exhausted. That's when they need to take time out, figure what's most important, and get their priorities straight. We also need to remember that God hasn't told us we have to do things alone. Sharing jobs and helping each other is what being members of the family of Christ is all about.

Turn to I Kings 19:2-18. **What did God do for Elijah first?** (Gave him food and let him rest.) **Why do you think He did that?** (Elijah's experiences on Mt. Carmel must have drained him physically and emotionally. God knows our physical weaknesses and wants us to value His gift of life by taking good care of ourselves.)

What did Elijah do after he had eaten and rested awhile? (Walked to Horeb, the mountain of God.) When Elijah first ran away he was so afraid he didn't pay attention to where he was going, but after regaining his physical health, he wanted to be near God and find a new purpose in life. He headed straight to the mountain where God had met with Moses and given the Ten Commandments. There he listened for God's voice. **When we are discouraged, we can follow Elijah's example and turn to the Lord. He is always near us and wants to help us. What are some ways we can hear God's voice today?** (Reading the Bible, going to Sunday school and church, sharing with Christian friends.)

God gave Elijah a new direction for his life by giving him different things to do for Him. Instead of being a busy leader as he had been before, now he was to anoint two new kings and train Elisha to be his replacement as God's representative to the people.

Direct the group's attention to verse 18. **How did God comfort Elijah?** (Told him there were seven thousand other believers who also worshiped Him.) **When we are**

lonely and think we're the only Christians around, remember that even if we don't know who or where they are, others are also faithfully living for God.**

Ask someone to look up Jeremiah 29:11 and read it aloud. **Would knowing this verse make a difference to someone who is very depressed? If so, why?** (Yes. This is a wonderful promise from God that He has good things in store for us. Instead of harm, He offers hope.) Instead of ending life in defeat, He offers a happy future. When people who feel that suicide is the only way to end their suffering are offered hope and a bright future they can choose life.

Have students read Romans 8:18 aloud together. Ask them to think of a statement that would be meaningful to them if they were enduring intense suffering. Choose one and let them add it to their Unit Verse "What to Do" booklets. You might select one like, "God is always near to help and comfort us."

✓ Living the Lesson (5-10 minutes)

Perhaps the most helpful thing we can do for those who feel life is meaningless is to show them we really care about them. Because our individual help may not be enough, we may need to involve other people. Who could we call on for additional help? (Parents or older brothers and sisters—yours or the troubled person's; adults you trust such as a youth leader, pastor, teacher, friend, school nurse, or family doctor.) Kids are often hesitant about involving adults, but point out that adults have more wisdom and authority and are thus better able to help.

Troubled kids often fear what their parents will think or say. In reality parents who really love their children often feel guilty because they wonder what they did to cause the pain which led to their child's problems.

Distribute the resource information sheet you prepared before class. Many people would rather stay in a bad situation than risk the unknown. To avoid this, tell them what happens when people get professional help—They are helped to find ways to lessen their emotional pain. Trained helpers aid them in understanding the experiences that led to the problem. They are encouraged to identify true feelings and express them freely which lessens the stress placed on them. Professionals help them find more positive ways to cope with their problems.

Close today's session by having kids hold hands but instead of forming a circle, have them form a heart. Close in prayer asking God to help you be more sensitive to others who feel depressed.

Read each sentence below and decide if it is TRUE or FALSE. If you think it is FALSE write a new sentence below it that is TRUE.

1. People who try suicide are weird. **TRUE** or **FALSE?**
   Rewrite:_____
   _____

2. Anyone who feels there is no hope or end to his/her pain may eventually think about suicide.
   TRUE or **FALSE?**
   Rewrite:_____
   _____

3. People who talk about suicide never really kill themselves. **TRUE** or **FALSE?**
   Rewrite:_____
   _____

4. People who are thinking about ending their lives usually give warning signs. **TRUE** or **FALSE?**
   Rewrite:_____
   _____

5. Talking to people about suicide will give them ideas about doing it. **TRUE** or **FALSE?**
   Rewrite:_____
   _____

6. People who have attempted to take their lives can be OK again after they have received hope
   and found helpful ways to handle their problems. **TRUE** or **FALSE?**
   Rewrite: _____
   _____

The Sighs That Bind

KID TOPPEL: Hello. My name is Kid Toppel and this is "Right Line." Today we're going to talk with two famous guests, Moses and Elijah. You men are known as great leaders who served God, yet you also endured great suffering and thought about death as a way out of your pain. When did that happen and how did you feel?

MOSES: While I was leading the Israelites through the wilderness to the promised land I became very discouraged. No matter what I did for them, it was never right. I was fed up with their complaints. I felt I just couldn't stand it any longer if they were going to act like this all the time. I was terribly lonely and felt hopeless.

ELIJAH: I know just how you felt. The Lord gave me a great victory over the false prophets of Baal and in answer to my prayer, He sent rain after three years of drought, but do you think anyone thanked me? No! Then evil Queen Jezebel threatened to kill me. No one stood up for me. I felt abandoned, empty, and beaten. Finally I ran away to the desert.

KID: How did each of you try to escape such terrible suffering?

MOSES: I talked to God about it. I told Him if He loved me, He would put me to death so I wouldn't have any more troubles.

ELIJAH: I talked to God too. I told Him I couldn't take it anymore and asked Him to let me die.

KID: Wow! You guys were desperate! Your experience makes me feel guilty because I haven't felt that way. How did your faith in God help you through this tough time?

MOSES: God showed me I wouldn't have to bear the burden alone. He gave me seventy helpers and promised that they would have the same spirit of prayer and loyalty to Him that I had.

ELIJAH: First God fed me and let me rest. Then He taught me how to shut out all the troubles around me and listen for His voice. That's when I realized His purpose for my life wasn't over yet. He even assured me that there were other faithful believers.

KID: What advice do you have for people who are discouraged and find life difficult?

MOSES: Remember that life is a gift from God. Show that you value it by looking for ways to enjoy it and using it to serve and honor God. Do what you can to help others value it, too.

ELIJAH: Because He gave it to you, God is the one who can best tell you how to spend your life. He has wonderful plans for you that can give you joy and satisfaction.

KID: Thank you for sharing with us today. As the Bible says, "This is the day the Lord has made; let us rejoice and be glad in it." This is Kid Toppel signing off for "Right Line."

Lesson 4

Heavenly Daze

Aim: That your students will understand what God's Word teaches us about life after death.

Scripture: I Corinthians 15:42-44; I Thessalonians 4:13-18

Unit Verse: I consider that our present sufferings are not worth comparing with the glory that will be revealed in us.
Romans 8:18

Unit Affirmation: I CAN GROW THROUGH PAINFUL EXPERIENCES!

 **Planning Ahead**

1. Photocopy Activity Sheets (pages 83 and 84)—one for each student.
2. Write these four "What Do You Think?" questions on separate pieces of paper and attach them to the wall in four separate areas of the room.
   WHAT HAPPENS WHEN A HUMAN BEING DIES?
   DOES IT HURT TO DIE? WHY OR WHY NOT?
   HOW CAN YOU TELL IF SOMETHING IS DEAD?
   WOULD IT BE POSSIBLE FOR SOMEONE OR SOMETHING TO COME ALIVE AFTER IT HAS DIED?

1 Setting the Stage (5-10 minutes)

WHAT YOU'LL DO

- Brainstorm some ideas and questions about death

WHAT YOU'LL NEED

- Four "What Do You Think?" questions
- Markers

2 Introducing the Issue (20 minutes)

WHAT YOU'LL DO

- Use an activity sheet to discuss beliefs people have about life after death
- Add a phrase to the Unit Affirmation poster

WHAT YOU'LL NEED

- "What Happens Then?" Activity Sheet (page 83)
- Unit Affirmation poster

3 Searching the Scriptures (20 minutes)

WHAT YOU'LL DO

- Discuss what God's Word teaches about life after death

WHAT YOU'LL NEED

- Two pieces of poster board or paper
- Unit Verse booklets

4 Living the Lesson (5-10 minutes)

WHAT YOU'LL DO

- Solve a puzzle that describes life after death

WHAT YOU'LL NEED

- "The Path of Life—Forever" Activity Sheet (page 84)

Lesson 4

 # Setting the Stage (5-10 minutes)

As students arrive, direct them to the "What Do You Think?" questions posted around the room. Have them write down some ideas about each question. Discuss these together. **Were there questions here that you have never thought about before? How did you know the answers to some of these questions?** Allow for responses.

Today we will be talking about beliefs people have about life after death and what the Bible teaches about this important topic.

 # Introducing the Issue (20 minutes)

If you could ask God to explain one thing about life after death to you, what would it be? Have students share questions. **The unknown is one reason death is so frightening. Because dead people can't come back to tell us about it, people have devised many theories of what happens after death.** Distribute copies of the activity sheet "What Happens Then?" (page 83). Have someone read the lead paragraph aloud. Work together to fill in the chart using the following information. Define the term "spirit." **The spirit is the real you. It is the part of you that feels happy when you obey God and sad when you don't. It is the part that tells God you love Him even when you don't talk out loud. Nobody can see your spirit, but your body is its earthly house. Your spirit never dies.**

Some people believe there is no life after death. There is only earthly life. When a person dies, spirit and body both die. The outcome was the same for everyone, good or evil. The Sadducees of Jesus' day held this belief. They also didn't believe in angels or demon spirits.

Reincarnation is the belief that after death the spirit goes into a body of another person or an animal. What you were like in your last life determines what you will be in your next life. The body dies and is never raised again. Those who believe this hope that the spirit works its way up to heaven by being better each lifetime. If you were good, you return higher in the social scale. If you were bad, you return worse and could be an animal or bug. When the spirit reaches perfection it returns to the dwelling place of its god. Ancient Greeks, Egyptians, and primitive people believed this as well as Buddhists and Hindus.

Heaven is God's special home. It is a place of joy where people who trusted in Jesus enjoy never-ending fellowship with God. Hell is Satan's

dwelling. It is a place of punishment for those who rejected God's salvation through Jesus. In hell these suffer a never-ending separation from God.

When Jesus was raised from the dead, He had a physical body as well as a spirit. This leads people to believe that both the body and soul live forever. Only Jesus died and lives to never die again. For that reason, we have to look to Him for guidance about life after death. Based on His example, Christians believe bodies and spirits are raised to never-ending life and spend eternity either in heaven or hell depending on what the people decided about Jesus in their earthly lives. Those who accepted His payment for sin by His death and followed Him, go to heaven. Others who rejected His salvation and lived for themselves go to hell.

Some religions teach that when people are not good enough to go to heaven and not wicked enough to go to hell, their bodies die and their spirits go to a place of temporary punishment called Purgatory. "Purgatory" comes from "purge" meaning to cleanse, purify, or remove [sins]. No one knows how long the spirit stays here or how much must be suffered because of individual differences. Going to heaven depends upon the prayers for them by people who are still alive. If they are delivered, their spirits and bodies are united in heaven. If not, in hell.

In order to grow through painful experiences we need to consider what God has to say about life after death. Display the Unit Affirmation poster and ask the group to read it aloud together. Then write the phrase, "because they force me to think about what is really important in life" on the fourth line. **Although no one has all the answers about life after death, God left us some clues in the Bible.**

☑ Searching the Scriptures (20 minutes)

Have students turn to I Corinthians 15:42-44. Write LIFE AFTER DEATH on the chalkboard or a large piece of paper. Divide the area into two columns and use the subtitles BEFORE and AFTER. **We're going to list all the facts this Scripture passage gives about life after death.** Have students take turns reading the passage aloud first. Let volunteers share their results and write their facts in the appropriate column. Cover the basic truths similar to the following:

BEFORE
- bodies die and decay
- bodies without honor

- bodies are weak
- bodies are natural/physical

AFTER

- bodies never die and decay
- bodies full of glory
- bodies have power
- bodies are spiritual.

Briefly review some of the special things Jesus could do after He rose again from death such as eat, speak, suddenly appear, disappear (even in rooms with locked doors), quickly reappear several miles away from where He was last seen. His new spiritual body no longer hurt or was weak but possessed new power.

Because Jesus was the first and only person to die and live again the Bible gives Him a special name. Have kids turn to Revelation 1:5 to find the term "firstborn from the dead." Jesus lives and will never die again.

Now ask the group to turn to I Thessalonians 4:13-18 and read it aloud as before. **How does the apostle Paul describe Christians who have died?** (They have fallen asleep.) Many kids first experience the reality of death when a favorite pet dies. It may have been explained to them that their pet just went to sleep and will never wake up again. Death is a little like falling asleep for people too, but unlike animals, people wake up again. This is the kind of analogy Paul makes in this passage.

Why do people who don't trust in Jesus have no hope? (Nothing to look forward to except darkness and separation from God; no future joys.) Use a different piece of paper to list the facts from these verses. Write THE LORD'S COMING at the top of the page. Volunteers can list the facts under this caption. Cover these basic truths:

- Jesus died and rose again
- God will bring with Jesus those followers who have died. Some followers will still be alive when Jesus comes down from heaven
- Loud command with voice of archangel (leader among God's angel-messengers) and trumpet call of God
- Dead in Christ will rise first
- Followers still alive will be caught up with them in the clouds to meet Lord in the air
- Christians will be with the Lord forever

How do you think these facts would encourage and comfort followers of Jesus who grieved over the death of another Christian? (Knew they would see them again, had a never-ending future of joy when they would be with them and Jesus forever.) **When a Christian dies, another Christian**

knows he only loses his friend for a while! His friend isn't lost because Jesus has promised Christians will be with Him in heaven!

Have students read Romans 8:18 aloud together. **When we are sad about the death of another follower of Jesus we can remember that these weak, decaying, natural bodies will be raised again someday and be new, spiritual bodies that are full of glory.** Let them suggest an appropriate sentence for their "What to Do" booklets that would comfort them when they grieve over a death. You can choose one like, "God gives us the hope of new, glorified bodies so we can live with Jesus forever." Have students take their booklets home at the end of class today.

✓ Living the Lesson (5-10 minutes)

The Bible tells us some things that will and won't be in heaven. Divide the class into two teams to look up different verses. Provide each team with a small slip of paper to record its conclusions. Team One will discover what is in heaven by checking out Psalm 16:11 while Team Two will make a list of what isn't in heaven by looking up Revelation 21:4. Select a secretary from each team to take notes and be prepared to share them with the group.

What are some things that won't be in heaven? (Death, mourning, crying, pain.) **Who will wipe away our tears?** (God.) **How does knowing these things make you feel?** (Happy, comforted, stronger to face suffering here on earth.)

What are some things that will be in heaven? (God, joy, eternal pleasures.)

Heaven is God's special home. Jesus was taken up to heaven after His resurrection. His disciples missed Him very much, but they were comforted by remembering a special promise He had made to them before His death on the cross. Read to your students John 14:1-3. **What did Jesus promise all those who are His followers?** (He would prepare a place for them in God's house, would come back and take them to with Him where He is in heaven.)

No one knows exactly when Jesus will come again. One thing we do know is that we need to be ready for His return. God has provided never-ending joyful life for those who trust Jesus and are His followers. But we don't have to wait until we die to begin our friendship with Him. We can start that today.

NOTE: Be sensitive to kids in your class who may not have received Jesus

as their Savior yet and who are wanting to make that decision. Help the student(s) to know who Jesus is and what He did on the cross, about Jesus' love for them, and their need for forgiveness. Have the student(s) pray with you. Scripture verses that would be helpful include: Romans 3:23, 5:8, 6:23, 10:9, 10.

Distribute copies of the activity sheet "The Path of Life" (page 84). **Jesus died to provide a full and rewarding life for us now. He promises that after death, we will have a joyful never-ending life with Him in heaven.** Allow time for kids to work on the puzzle or complete it at home.

Close by giving thanks to God for turning our suffering and pain into final triumph and glory with the reassurance of joyous life with Him forever.

What Happens Then?

Death is a fearful thing to many people because they wonder what happens next. There are some big differences between what people believe and what the Bible teaches. Knowing the difference can be a matter of endless life or endless death! Fill in the answers to the questions during the class discussion.

1. NO LIFE AFTER DEATH

What happens to the spirit? _____

What happens to the body? _____

How is the outcome decided? _____

2. REINCARNATION

What happens to the spirit? _____

What happens to the body? _____

How is the outcome decided? _____

3. A SPIRITUAL AND BODILY LIFE IN HEAVEN OR HELL

What happens to the spirit? _____

What happens to the body? _____

How is the outcome decided? _____

4. PURGATORY

What happens to the spirit? _____

What happens to the body? _____

How is the outcome decided? _____

The Path of Life—Forever

Read these verses that explain about life after death. Then write the underlined words in the appropriate spaces in the puzzle.

"<u>Jesus</u> said to <u>her</u>, 'I am the <u>resurrection</u> and the <u>life</u>. He who <u>believes</u> in me <u>will</u> live, even <u>though</u> he dies; and <u>whoever</u> <u>lives</u> and believes in me will <u>never</u> <u>die</u>." John 11:25, 26

"In my <u>Father's</u> <u>house</u> are <u>many</u> <u>rooms</u>; if it were not so, I would have told you. I am going <u>there</u> to <u>prepare</u> a <u>place</u> for <u>you</u>. And if I go and prepare a place for you, I will <u>come</u> back and take you to be with <u>me</u> that you <u>also</u> may be where I am." John 14:2, 3

Service Projects for Pain & Death

In addition to the projects listed in these lessons, your class or church can also serve in the following ways:

✔ 1. Design a book of appropriate Scripture verses for kids to keep and use with those who are suffering or grieving. You could copy the verses and illustrate them. Include paraphrases of these verses by having your class members rewrite them in a simplified version for kids their own age.

✔ 2. Help organize a prayer chain for members of the church family who experience pain or loss. If your church already has a prayer chain, students can publicize it so everyone is aware of it and have access to it in times of need.

✔ 3. Visit a support group. Most localities have some form of these such as Chronic Pain, Teen-Anon, or Compassionate Friends. Observe how these groups strengthen their members by sharing mutual experiences.

✔ 4. Form a support group for kids enduring painful ordeals. Since hope is the big weapon against a feeling of helplessness, suffering kids desperately need to know they are not alone. They need to know that others have endured and overcome the same trials they are going through. With God's guidance, your students can help one another cope with pain.

✔ 5. Visit a local crisis center. Check with your pastor for names and addresses of these agencies. If an organization does not allow visitors, ask for any educational information they can provide.

 *Junior* Electives

Heroes for Today . . .

Think back to when you were ten or eleven years old. Who were the heroes you admired? Was it a famous baseball star, a singer, an Olympic athlete, or a local high school football hero? Maybe you looked up to a world leader or a favorite teacher at school! How about today? No matter what our age, we all have heroes we admire and want to emulate.

Today's heroes for your Juniors range from cartoon characters like Bart Simpson to talented athletic stars like Michael Jordan. As in our experience, their heroes include astronauts, actors, musicians as well as teachers, coaches, and other community leaders, both men and women, young and old. However, kids today are bombarded with confusing messages about the role of heroes in their lives. Media, especially, has clouded the issue. Companies pay huge sums of money to get celebrity endorsements to help sell their products. Newspapers and magazines detail every movement of the "hot, popular" stars. As a result, although some of today's heroes still model moral, caring lives that make a difference, others make drugs, alcohol, and "life in the fast lane" look like an appealing and a desirable lifestyle.

In the weeks ahead, your students will have an opportunity to learn how the heroes they choose can influence their lives, both positively and negatively. They will also look for places and ways they can become heroes to others around them. Most importantly, however, they will see how Jesus is the timeless hero we can follow and trust to set the perfect example! You will have the joy of inviting your students to choose Jesus as their own #1 hero and example for a lifetime!

Hero Worship Overview

Unit Verse: Join with others in following my example, brothers, and take note of those who live according to the pattern we gave you. Philippians 3:17

Unit Affirmation: I CAN HAVE HEROES TO ADMIRE AND RESPECT!

LESSON	TITLE	OBJECTIVE	SCRIPTURE BASE
Lesson #1	Who's My Hero?	That your students will define what makes a hero and identify the ones to whom they relate.	Acts 23:12-35
Lesson #2	Follow the Leader	That your students will understand the heroes they choose may affect the directions their lives take.	II Kings 22:1-11, 13; 23:1-3, 15, 25
Lesson #3	Quality You Can Count On!	That your students will learn how patterning their lives after godly heroes can make them heroes to others.	II Kings 5:1-14
Lesson #4	Everybody Needs This Hero	That your students will identify Jesus as the ideal hero and choose to follow Him, patterning their lives after His example.	Philippians 2:5-11

Partners

*F*or the next few weeks your Junior-age child will be part of a group learning about Heroes. *Partners* is a planned parent piece to keep you informed of what will be taught during this exciting series.

PREVIEW...

Heroes

Think back to when you were ten or eleven years old. Who were the heroes you looked up to? Was it a famous baseball star, a singer, an Olympic athlete, or a local high school football hero? Maybe you looked up to a world leader or a favorite teacher at school! How about today? No matter what our age, we all have and need heroes to respect and emulate.

Heroes for today's Juniors range from cartoon characters like Bart Simpson to talented athletic stars like Michael Jordan. As in our experience, their heroes include astronauts, actors, musicians as well as teachers, coaches, and other community leaders, both men and women, young and old.

However, kids today are bombarded with confusing messages about the role of heroes in their lives. Media, especially, has clouded the issue. Companies pay huge sums of money to get celebrity endorsements to sell their products. Newspapers and magazines detail every movement of the "hot, popular" stars. As a result, although some of today's heroes still model moral, caring lives that make a difference, others make drugs, alcohol, and "life in the fast lane" look like an appealing and desirable lifestyle.

During this unit, your child(ren) will have an opportunity to learn how the heroes they choose can influence their lives, both positively and negatively. They will also look for places and ways they can become heroes to others around them. As they review the Unit Affirmation and Unit Verse each week, they will be encouraged to look for godly heroes and to pattern their lives after these people. Finally, after making some evaluations about the heroes the world has to offer, they will be challenged to make Jesus their #1 hero; the perfect hero to serve

as a pattern for each one of us!

Unit Verse:

Join with others in following my example, brothers, and take note of those who live according to the pattern we gave you. Philippians 3:17

Unit Affirmation:

I CAN HAVE HEROES TO ADMIRE AND RESPECT!

PRINCIPLES...

Heroes

This unit will help Juniors understand several aspects regarding heroes. They are:

PRINCIPLE #1: REAL HEROES ARE BASED ON ACTIONS AND CHARACTER; NOT ON MEDIA "HYPE."

The media has incredible power to "make" heroes. Many of today's popular personalities are known because of clever publicity campaigns designed to make money, not promote positive role models for kids. Early on, our children must learn to differentiate between media "hype" and real heroes

they can look up to because of wise choices, solid reputations, and godly achievements. The first step in choosing a role model or hero is the ability to make this distinction.

PRINCIPLE #2:
HEROES PROVIDE A PATTERN AND EXAMPLE FOR EVERYDAY LIVING.

Junior-age children are very observant. They watch closely the behaviors of those they admire most! The heroes they choose have a direct influence on the choices they make each day. Heroes worth following provide examples of good living skills that will assist your child(ren) in handling the daily life situations they face every day.

PRINCIPLE #3:
I CAN BE A HERO, TOO.

The subject of heroes is not a one way street. Our kids need to realize that not only are their lives shaped by the heroes they choose, but they have others in their lives who look up to them! Even Junior-age children can serve as role models to those around them. During this unit, your children will be challenged to look for specific places and actions that can help them serve as role models for others. They will be encouraged to pattern their lives after godly people, so that they in turn can be godly examples to others.

PRINCIPLE #4:
JESUS IS THE PERFECT HERO!

The ultimate role model for any Christian is Jesus Christ. Your child will survey the characteristics Jesus displayed that set Him apart as the ideal hero and then have an opportunity to make Jesus their #1 hero! They will also be challenged to continue following their #1 hero by obeying His words and considering His example through all of life.

PRACTICE...

Heroes

You can reinforce what your child is learning in this unit by doing one or more of these at-home activities:

1. RESEARCH HISTORICAL HEROES TOGETHER.

Take time to visit the library and choose a biography about a hero of interest to your family. Read the book together and discuss how this person impacted those around him or her. Look for qualities and characteristics in that hero that serve as valuable patterns your child can follow.

2. HIDE GOD'S WORD IN YOUR HEARTS.

Memorize the Unit Verse together as a family. Meal time is a good time to say it together and talk about its meaning for each family member.

3. CATCH A HERO IN ACTION!

Look for behaviors and examples to reward within your family each day. Choose a time to name a "hero of the day" and talk about why that person was chosen. Some examples are: sharing, watching out for someone else, obeying, setting a good example, making a wise decision. Let each person in the family have a chance both to pick a hero and to be a hero!

4. DISCOVER THE PERFECT HERO

Do a word study on the different names for Jesus. Using a concordance or other resource book, pick a different name for Jesus each day and talk about the characteristics of a hero Jesus displays, as represented in that name.

5. LOOK FOR EVERYDAY HEROES.

Most local newspapers routinely carry stories about heroes. Look for articles describing ordinary people who perform heroic feats. Share them together and discuss the circumstances surrounding the event. What examples can you find in these accounts that can influence the everyday lives of your family members?

Lesson 1

Who's My Hero?

Aim: That your students will define what makes a hero and identify the ones to whom they relate.

Scripture: Acts 23:12-35

Unit Verse: Join with others in following my example, brothers, and take note of those who live according to the pattern we gave you. Philippians 3:17

Unit Affirmation: I CAN HAVE HEROES TO ADMIRE AND RESPECT!

Planning Ahead

1. Photocopy Activity Sheets (pages 94 and 95)—one for each student.
2. Cut 15 strips of poster board or paper approximately 6" x 22".
3. Label five lunch bags with the following words: POLITICAL/NATIONAL, BIBLE, SPORTS, ENTERTAINMENT, and OTHER.
4. Prepare the Unit Affirmation poster by writing across the top of a large poster board the sentence I CAN HAVE HEROES TO ADMIRE AND RESPECT! Under the title, write the numbers 1-5 vertically down the left-hand side.
5. Prepare the following title for Unit Verse bulletin board: BE A HERO . . . Divide the board into four sections with yarn or narrow strips of paper. Prepare the materials for section one: a picture of a home and family with the word HOME written in large print; and the words of I Peter 3:8 written on a large piece of paper.
6. Prepare "Heroes for Today" cards as described in LIVING THE LESSON.
7. Ask one or two non-class members to assist during class today to tabulate survey results.

1 Setting the Stage (5-10 minutes)

WHAT YOU'LL DO

- Conduct a survey to discover the top heroes

WHAT YOU'LL NEED

- "Who's Who of Heroes" Activity Sheet (page 94)

2 Introducing the Issue (20 minutes)

WHAT YOU'LL DO

- Play a game to summarize results of the survey
- Form a definition for the word "hero"
- Introduce the Unit Affirmation poster

WHAT YOU'LL NEED

- Compiled survey results
- 3 or 4 dictionaries and a thesaurus
- Unit Affirmation poster
- **OPTIONAL:** A copy of *Reader's Digest* magazine's feature article, "Heroes for Today"

3 Searching the Scripture (20 minutes)

WHAT YOU'LL DO

- Use an activity sheet to dramatize a story of a Bible hero who saved Paul's life
- Discuss being a hero at home

WHAT YOU'LL NEED

- "Nephew to the Rescue!" Activity Sheet (page 96)
- Unit Verse bulletin board

4 Living the Lesson (5-10 minutes)

WHAT YOU'LL DO

- Play a game to identify "everyday heroes" in our lives

WHAT YOU'LL NEED

- "Heroes for Today" cards

Lesson 1

Setting the Stage (5-10 minutes)

As children arrive today, distribute copies of the activity sheet "Who's Who of Heroes" (page 95). Welcome them to the room by explaining that for the next four weeks you will be talking about heroes. To get ready for this unit, they are to write the names of the people they admire most for each category listed: Political/National leaders, Sports, Bible, Entertainment, and Other. Then they are to cut apart the slips and put each one in the bag labeled with the corresponding category title. IMPORTANT! Since the results of this survey will be used in a game during INTRODUCING THE ISSUE, impress on your students the need to keep their answers to themselves. They may need to discuss possible names to get some ideas, but their votes should be kept secret.

Ask your guest assistants to tabulate the results of the survey and prepare them for use in the game. When all the votes are in, they are to record the top three heroes named in each category and write each name on a separate strip of cardboard. Attach these strips to the wall (with the writing facing the wall so it cannot be read), making a separate column for each category.

How many of you had an easy time thinking of heroes? How many had a hard time? Let kids respond. **Which categories did you find easiest? Hardest?** Allow for responses. **We all have heroes in our lives. As we look at heroes over the next few weeks, we're going to talk about who our heroes are and why we value them. We will also think about what effect, if any, they have on our everyday lives. In a few minutes we will see who your heroes are. First, let's think about what a "hero" is.**

Introducing the Issue (20 minutes)

Let's come up with a definition of what a hero really is. Divide the class into groups of four or five. Have at least one dictionary and a thesaurus available. Give each group time to come up with a definition without copying from the dictionary. Suggest they make a list of words to describe what a hero is and a list of words to describe what a hero is not. Bring the class together to review their answers, and summarize their comments on the board.

Webster's Dictionary defines a hero as: A person of exceptional quality who wins admiration by noble deeds, especially deeds of courage. Can be either male or female, living or dead, real or imaginary, young or old. Some synonyms are: champion, superstar, or idol. Using ideas from the kids, agree on an overall definition of the word.

What's on your list of the qualities a hero might have? Brainstorm as long a list of qualities as possible. Examples are: leader, wise, talented, brave, hardworking,

make good choices, good sense of humor, fearless. Some words to describe what a hero is not are: unreliable, disregards others, gives up. **Now that we know a little more about what a hero is, let's take a look at the heroes you listed in your surveys. Let's play "Who's Who of Heroes".**

NOTE: By now, your helpers should have completed their compilation of the survey results and taped the cardboard strips containing the top three responses in each category to the wall. Have them give you a list of the winning names to use as you lead the game.

The goal of our game is to guess which "heroes" got the most votes in our survey. Divide the class into two teams. If your class is small play together as one group. Choose four people from one team to go first. They will each get to guess one person they think is on the list in each category. Other team members may confer to help the players guessing. When they guess correctly, turn that cardboard strip over so it can be read, and award points: 100 for the top answer, 75 for the second, and 50 for the third. If those four children are unable to guess all three answers, the other team gets a chance to guess the remaining answers. Keep the game moving quickly so you can get through all five categories. When the game is over, lead a discussion about the people named in the survey.

We had fun learning a little about who we named as our top heroes, but now let's think about our choices. Based on our definition of a hero and the characteristics we think a hero has or has not, let's look at these names again. Which ones fit well with our understanding of a hero? Are there ones that don't fit? What's the difference? Allow for discussion of this point. Direct the kids to think about the difference between people who are truly heroes, and those who are famous but do not have heroic behavior or attitudes. **Just because a person or character is known by us does not mean he or she is a suitable hero for us to follow. Which people on our list have been heroes a long time? Why do you think they have been heroes so long?** Allow for responses. Real heroes are based on actions and character that stand the test of time. **Let's look at our list one more time. Are there some names we could eliminate? Are there others we can add?** Direct their thoughts by suggesting some categories: doctors, explorers, scientists.

There is one more point we need to make about heroes. Does a person have to be famous to be a hero? It is important for the kids to understand that heroes come in all shapes, sizes, and stations in life. It is *character* that makes a hero, not visibility.

OPTIONAL: *Reader's Digest* magazine has a feature article entitled "Heroes for Today." Each month it highlights three or four ordinary people who are named

as heroes for a variety of reasons. You might consider reading an excerpt from these articles each week during this unit.

Introduce the Unit Affirmation poster by displaying it in a place where everyone can see it. Read it aloud together. Fill in the first line by asking the kids to suggest phrases to summarize their definition of a hero. Sample phrases are "A hero is a person of exceptional quality," or "A hero is someone I would like to be like." Choose one and write it on line one. **Heroes come in all shapes, sizes, and ages! Let's look at a little known young Bible hero who made a big difference in the life of the apostle Paul.**

Searching the Scriptures (20 minutes)

We said earlier that one definition of a hero is someone known for exceptional deeds of courage. Today's story is about a boy who showed courage. We don't even know the name of this young man, but his "deed of courage" saved the apostle Paul from death!

Distribute copies of the activity sheet "Nephew to the Rescue" (page 96) to each student and assign class members to be the characters in the drama. If you have a large class, you might want to do the drama twice so more kids can have a chance to participate. When you have finished, discuss what happened next in this story. Create five groups and give each group one of the following Scripture references to look up: Acts 23:23, Acts 23:23, Acts 23:23, Acts 23:25, Acts 23:33-35. They are to read their reference and be prepared to respond with the appropriate questions when you give the following answers.

1. **The answer is 200. What is the question?** (How many soldiers were assigned to accompany Paul?)

2. **The answer if 70. What is the question?** (How many horsemen were assigned to accompany Paul?)

3. **The answer is 200. What is the question?** (How many spearmen were assigned to accompany Paul?)

4. **The answer is write a letter. What is the question?** (What did the commander do next?)

5. **The answer is "I will hear your case when your accusers get here." What is the question?** (What did the governor say when he received the Commander's letter?)

Fortunately, the story does have a happy ending! The soldiers carried out their duties by taking Paul with them during the night. With such a large military unit, the assassins thought it was just a regular group of soldiers out on military maneuvers. They never dreamed Paul was in their ranks! The

group reached Caesarea and handed him over to the governor, Felix. Paul was held in protective custody pending trial, but the immediate danger of the assassination plot was over! Paul's life was saved, thanks to the courage of one boy!

How many of you had ever heard that story before? Allow for responses. **Do you think Paul's nephew ever dreamed the story of his actions that night would end up recorded in the Bible and be read by people almost 2,000 years later? Probably not. But his courage and strength saved Paul and allowed God to continue His plan for one of the most important times in Paul's life!**

Share with the class that this is the first time any member of Paul's family is mentioned in the Bible. Some scholars wonder if there might have been some disagreements in the family. It is very likely that Paul's conversion to the Christian faith caused the rest of Paul's family to disown him. (In that time, that meant treating him as if he were dead; any contact with him would have been strictly forbidden.) There is a good possibility that Paul's sister and her son continued to worship with the Jews, not the Jewish Christians, which would explain how his nephew might have had access to the death threat. It also means that the risk he took to go to Paul would have been even greater, since he was forbidden to speak to his uncle.

How do you think Paul's nephew felt when he overheard the death plot? (Scared, anxious, confused.) **What were some of the choices he could have made?** (Ignored the whole thing; told his mother; joined the plan.) Spend some time making a long list of possibilities. **What were some of the risks involved in going to the prison?** (He might have been imprisoned, too. They might not have let him in to see Paul. One of the assassins might have followed him and killed him, too.) **What risks did he take in going to the Commander?** (He might have put him in prison. He could have laughed at him and told him he was young and inexperienced.) **Why do you think the Commander asked him not to tell anyone?** (To assure secrecy and keep the information quiet.) **Do you think it was easy to keep the information quiet?** (Probably not; he would have wanted to tell his story to everyone!) **What might have happened if he had not respected the need for secrecy?** (The assassins could have heard about the Commander's plan and they would have found a different way to kill Paul.) **What facts make it clear that the Commander knew the threat was real?** (His response, the number of troops sent with Paul, and the speed at which he responded to the threat; the fact that they moved at night.)

God used Paul's nephew to change the course of events that night. Why do you think it was so important for Paul's life to be spared? (God still had much for Paul to accomplish.) **God had many more plans for Paul! In the days that followed, Paul spent a great deal of time in prison and on trial, but through it all he was able to tell his story over and over. He told many people, both Romans and Jews how he had been blinded on the road to**

Damascus and how Jesus had made a real difference in his life! Think of all that would have never happened if Paul's nephew had not acted so bravely. Think back to our definition of a hero. Do you think Paul's nephew qualifies? Why or Why not? This boy did live according to God's plan. He was bold and honest. It took great courage, and God used this young boy to protect His servant and spread His Good News!

Introduce the Unit Verse by having the kids find Philippians 3:17 in their Bibles and reading the verse together. Then read the verse again, using the following motions to help them remember it. When the verse says, "Join with others," have them grab a friend's hand. When the verse says, "and take note of those who live according to the pattern we gave you," have them hold out a hand as if they had a small notepad in it and pretend to write on it with the other hand.

Our Unit Verse tells us that we are to follow the example of others who live for the Lord. Each week, for the next four weeks, when we review the Unit Verse, we will look at a different place we can follow God's plan. This week we'll talk about being a hero at home. Refer to the Unit Verse bulletin board and add the picture or word "Home." Then ask kids to find I Peter 3:8 and read it together. What would it be like to live in a home where everyone lived according to this commandment? What can you do to be a hero at home? Allow for responses. Sometimes it's hardest to be a hero at home. Why do you think that might be? (We spend the most time there. It's a place where we can relax and be ourselves.) What characteristics are listed in this verse that a hero might have? (Sympathetic, loving, compassionate, humble, gets along with others.) This week as you think about heroes, work at being a hero in your own home. Use this verse as your base everyday in deciding how you will treat those around you at home.

Living the Lesson (5-10 minutes)

Before class, prepare eight to twelve 3" x 5" cards with the names of familiar occupations on each one. Suggestions: pastor, dentist, teacher, parent, astronaut.

Most of the heroes we've talked about today have been celebrities or famous people, but you don't have to be famous to be a hero. People you see in your community everyday can be heroes too. Let's play a game to identify heroes in our lives. Divide the class into two teams. Choose one team to go first and give them a "Heroes for Today" card. They have one minute to act out the profession. When a word is guessed, ask: Why might this person be considered a hero? What qualities would he or she need?

Close today's session by thanking God for giving us heroes to look up to. Encourage the kids to be on the "lookout" for heroes this week!

Who's Who of Heroes

POLITICAL/NATIONAL LEADERS:

1ST CHOICE _____

2ND CHOICE _____

3RD CHOICE _____

ENTERTAINMENT HEROES:

1ST CHOICE _____

2ND CHOICE _____

3RD CHOICE _____

SPORTS HEROES:

1ST CHOICE _____

2ND CHOICE _____

3RD CHOICE _____

BIBLE HEROES:

1ST CHOICE _____

2ND CHOICE _____

3RD CHOICE _____

OTHER HEROES—ANY CATEGORY:

1ST CHOICE _____

2ND CHOICE _____

3RD CHOICE _____

Nephew to the Rescue!

NARRATOR: Today we are going to travel to the city of Jerusalem and look in on the Apostle Paul. Once again, we find him sitting in jail, a very unpleasant place to be! This time, however, things are worse than ever before. There is growing hatred for Paul because his teachings have the whole city in an uproar. Even though he is in jail, many men in power are not willing to let it rest. The situation here tonight is tense, to say the least!

PAUL: Prison is definitely not my favorite place to be! But at least I'm getting a lot of letters written and keeping up on my correspondence.

NEPHEW: (Runs in, out of breath.) Uncle Paul, I'm so glad I found you. You're in great danger. I was at my friend's house . . .

PAUL: Wait a minute . . . slow down! How did you get in here? Do you know what could happen if you are caught? You have to leave . . . .

NEPHEW: But Uncle Paul, you have to hear this! When I was at John Luke's house I overheard something. There were so many men there, at least 40! What they said scared me so much I came right here.

PAUL: What's going on son?

NEPHEW: Well, this is what I heard . . . .

JEW #1: We've got to kill him! He's nothing but trouble!

JEW #2: That's for sure. But he's in prison. How can we possibly get to him?

JEW #3: There's got to be a way! We'll just have to think!

JEW #4: Well, I make a motion that none of us eat or drink until Paul is dead!

GROUP: Yes! No food! Nothing to drink! We make an oath that nothing will pass our lips until Paul is dead!

JEW #1: If we could only get Paul out of the prison and into the streets! Then we could just overpower the guard and kill Paul.

JEW #2: What if we ask the Sanhedrin to request an inquiry? They will ask a commander to transport him. We'll hide in the streets and kill him before he ever reaches the inquiry.

JEW #5: Yes! A brilliant idea! We can do it! We'll be eating and drinking in no time!

GROUP: All for one and one for all. To Paul's death!

PAUL: Are you in danger? Did they see you?

NEPHEW: I think they might have seen me run away from the house. But I had to tell you! We have to do something!

PAUL: Well, I could . . . . But, no! It's too risky. If they did see you, they are probably following you and there is no telling what they will do to you if you get any more involved!

NEPHEW: What? Tell me what to do! If you don't, I'll go to the Commander myself, I promise I will!

PAUL: OK, I give up! And, whatever happens, I will always be grateful for your help! Guard! Take this young man to the Commander; he has something to tell him.

GUARD: Come along with me, boy!

COMMANDER: Guard, who is this young boy you bring to me?

GUARD: It's Paul's nephew. He says he has important information for you.

COMMANDER: What is it, boy? You seem so scared!

NEPHEW: (speaking very quickly) There are over 40 men who are planning to kill my Uncle Paul and you've just got to stop them . . .

COMMANDER: Hold on! Slow down! Just tell me their plan.

NEPHEW: (takes a deep breath) They are going to hide and wait for him when he is taken to the inquiry at the Sanhedrin. On the way they are going to ambush him and kill him. I heard them bragging about how it would be a piece of barley cake!

COMMANDER: Well, we'll see about that! Go home now and don't breathe a word of this to anyone!

NARRATOR: This is an interesting turn of events. The book of Acts tells us how the story ends. You can read it for yourself in Acts 23:12-35.

Lesson 2

Follow the Leader

Aim: That your students will understand that the heroes they choose may affect the directions their lives take.

Scripture: II Kings 22:1-11, 13; 23:1-3, 15, 25

Unit Verse: Join with others in following my example, brothers, and take note of those who live according to the pattern we gave you. Philippians 3:17

Unit Affirmation: I CAN HAVE HEROES TO ADMIRE AND RESPECT!

 **Planning Ahead**

1. Photocopy Activity Sheets (pages 103 and 104)—one for each student.
2. Prepare Leader Instruction cards for the Follow the Leader game. Write each of the following words or phrases on a separate card: skip, jump, march, shake all over, hop like a bunny, take baby steps, take giant steps, walk singing "Row, Row, Row Your Boat" as loud as you can, flap your arms like a bird. Make enough cards so each child will have one.
3. Prepare the following materials for the Unit Verse bulletin board: a picture of a school or the word SCHOOL written in large letters, the words of I Corinthians 16:13, 14 written on a large piece of paper.
4. Ask parents and other teachers to help you prepare a list of the sports figures, TV personalities, musicians, and other individuals who are especially popular with your group of students.

1 Setting the Stage (5-10 minutes)

WHAT YOU'LL DO

- Play Follow the Leader to experience leading and following

WHAT YOU'LL NEED

- Leader Instruction cards

2 Introducing the Issue (20 minutes)

WHAT YOU'LL DO

- Use an activity sheet to identify the influence of heroes
- Discuss ways heroes have both negative and positive influences
- Add a phrase to the Unit Affirmation poster

WHAT YOU'LL NEED

- "Circles of Influence" Activity Sheet (page 103)
- Unit Affirmation poster

3 Searching the Scriptures (20 minutes)

WHAT YOU'LL DO

- Use an activity sheet to discover how one heroic king proved to be a great influence
- Discuss being a hero at school

WHAT YOU'LL NEED

- "Josiah's Royal Legacy" Activity Sheet (page 104)
- Unit Verse bulletin board

4 Living the Lesson (5-10 minutes)

WHAT YOU'LL DO

- Describe a legacy to leave here on earth

WHAT YOU'LL NEED

- "Josiah's Royal Legacy" Activity Sheet (page 104)

✓ Setting the Stage (5-10 minutes)

When three or four students have arrived, begin a game of Follow the Leader. Incorporate other students into the game as soon as they enter your room. Begin the game yourself or ask a helper to take the lead and enthusiastically lead the group in several bold, unusual movements and even a few silly ones. Then let one of your class members take over as leader by choosing an instruction card and leading the others in the activity described.

> **OPTIONAL:** If weather permits, take the group outside to play this game.
> Have each child take a turn being the leader for approximately 30 to 60 seconds, using a card describing the movements to lead. When as many as possible have experienced being the leader, gather the group together for a time of discussion.

Many of you had a turn to lead the others. What did it feel like? Give students an opportunity to respond. **Did you like feeling in charge and in control? Why or why not? How did it feel to be responsible for the others following you?**

One of the characteristics many heroes have is leadership ability. Many heroes are trendsetters and have a big influence over those around them. Today we're going to look at how the heroes we choose in our lives have a direct influence in shaping our lives.

✓ Introducing the Issue (20 minutes)

How many of you think you are influenced by people you admire? Have you ever heard the term "hero worship"? What do you think it means? Allow for responses. **When people use that phrase they usually mean that someone is totally in awe of a hero or role model. They may study the way they look, act, talk, and live. Most of us don't go to quite those extremes, but the people we admire and look up to can definitely influence our behavior and decisions. Let's see some specific ways this might happen.**

Distribute copies of the activity sheet "Circles of Influence" (page 103). **We're going to use this activity sheet to begin thinking about ways we allow people we admire to influence us. The term "sphere (or circle) of influence" can be defined as a limited area within which something is effective. We all have "spheres of influence" in our lives. Those are the areas in which we let other people affect the way we speak, act, dress**

Lesson 2

and think. Complete this form by thinking about the people who influence you everyday.

As your kids work individually, circulate among them to assist those who may need it. Use your prepared list of popular personalities to make suggestions if appropriate. For example, many of your students might save for months just to buy the same brand of shoes that one of their favorite sports heroes wears. Others use phrases and expressions that come directly from cartoon characters or TV personalities. Also remind them their answers don't necessarily have to be famous people. Teachers, parents, siblings or friends influence us, too.

After a few minutes, give them a chance to share their answers. **Look at your lists and let's talk about some of the people that have an influence on you. What are some of the positive things you've learned from heroes in your life?** Allow for responses. **Are all the people on your list famous? Do some of them live in your own house? Are there some phrases you say because everyone else at school is saying them? What shoes or clothes are "in" and which aren't? Who sets the standard of acceptability for these?** Allow for responses.

We said heroes can have a great influence on the way people act and think, some positively and some negatively. Have you ever been disappointed by something a hero did or said? Can you think of some examples of heroes who have had a negative influence in some way? (Some popular musicians and TV stars take drugs or abuse alcohol, Pete Rose was convicted of gambling, some athletes take steroids, Richard Nixon didn't tell the truth about Watergate, some people might lie or cheat on their income taxes, some make jokes at the expense of others or use foul language.) Point out that heroes can bring out the best or worst in us. Some might use drugs or alcohol. Others may use bad language or lie. If we admire that person, we may think those actions are cool too, and adopt them as a part of our life style. We like to do as our heroes do, no matter what.

Why do we need to be careful about who we pick as heroes? (Not everyone uses the Bible and its commandments on which to base their actions and ideas.) **Does this mean a person has to be perfect to be a hero?** (No.) Remind your class that each one of the people mentioned had many positive things to offer, too. They each had a talent or experience that could serve as an excellent role model. But we must carefully choose our heroes and then carefully choose in what way to be like them—or not. Remember that they are not perfect. We can follow some of their leading, and reject other characteristics that are not helpful to us.

Display the Unit Affirmation poster and have the class read the affirmation

aloud together. Add a phrase to sum up today's discussion. Suggest the following phrases and let the kids vote on which one they like best: "Heroes influence my life", "Heroes can bring out the best or worst in me", or "Heroes I choose can determine how I live my life." Record the winner on the poster. **As we said last week, heroes don't need to be adults. Many young people are heroes. Today we are going to see how another young boy in the Bible served as a king and influenced a whole nation by his actions. Let's look at this example of a godly hero!**

Searching the Scriptures (20 minutes)

Do any of you know what the word *LEGACY* means? Explain that a legacy is something someone leaves behind when they die. It's usually money, property, an action or event. It's an account of how someone influenced the environment or people around them. **Today we are going to learn about a king who left a great legacy. Can you imagine becoming a king at the age of eight? All of you would be experienced royalty already! Would you feel qualified or capable of running a kingdom? A parallel would be to think of becoming the leader of a very large country like ours when you are only eight years old! That's exactly what happened to Josiah. He was the sixteenth king of Judah and one of the most godly kings in the Old Testament. When he took control, Jerusalem was a mess! The people were worshiping idols, and building altars to pagan gods. The temple was in shambles because no one ever went there to worship the Lord anymore. Worship of the Lord was practically nonexistent. In fact they couldn't even find the copy of the Book of the Law (the Bible of that time) in the temple! Let's take a look at what Josiah did to turn things around.**

Distribute copies of the activity sheet "Josiah's Royal Legacy" (page 104). Do all but the last section now. The Bible is clear in describing Josiah as one of the most influential and godly kings! As you review the sheet together point out that:

1. Age did not hold back Josiah. He became king at the age of eight and steadily worked to make things better in his kingdom.

2. He did not follow the example of his father and grandfather, who were among the worst of the kings in Judah's history. Rather, he put in motion a plan to clean up the city of Jerusalem and the temple, and get the people back to worshiping God.

3. His course was steady and true. Even though he was young, he made many important decisions. He knew what was right and what God expected

Lesson 2

him to do, and he determined that no one would keep him from doing it!

We can see that Josiah was no ordinary king! He influenced thousands of people in positive ways! He was definitely a hero in the truest sense! Do you think his job was an easy one? Why or why not? How might things have been different if Josiah had chosen the ways of his father and grandfather? (The people of Jerusalem would have continued in their wicked ways. The Book of the Law would not have been recovered nor the temple restored.)

Display a copy of the Unit Verse. Ask if anyone can remember the hand motions you used last week to help remember the verse. ("Join with others"—take the hand of a friend. "Take note of those who live"—pretend to write on an imaginary notepad in your hand.) Say the verse together several times. **This verse certainly describes the life of Josiah! He set a super example for his people and lived according to God's law. What qualities do you admire most about Josiah?** Allow for responses. **If we were really taking notes on who we should follow, Josiah's name would definitely have to be on the list. He left a long list of accomplishments for the Lord and his people. What examples can we learn and follow from Josiah?** (Don't think that just because you're young you can't accomplish anything for the Lord. Live your life so that you can influence others to learn more about God.)

Last week we talked about one place we can all be heroes. Who remembers where that was? (Home.) Direct their attention to the Unit Bulletin Board and review last week's command to help us be heroes at home. **This week we're going to add another place where we can be heroes to others in our everyday lives.** Add a picture or the word "School" to the bulletin board.

What can you do to be a hero at school? It's not always easy to set an example at school. What things make standing up for what you believe and doing what is right difficult at school? (Worrying what others will think, pressure of grades and expectations, fear of not fitting in with friends.) Attach the poster of the command verses, I Corinthians 16:13,14 "Be on your guard; stand firm in the faith; be men of courage; be strong. Do everything in love." **These verses certainly describe the way Josiah lived his life. He was on guard against the false gods and teachings of his land and had the courage to destroy them. He stood firm in the faith even when he was only eight years old and continued to lead others in the faith throughout his lifetime. His motivation for all of this was his love for the Lord and for the people of his kingdom. Who are some heroes at school who can influence you appropriately?** (Friends, other classmates, teachers.) **Who are not appropriate heroes?** (Those involved in things like

cheating, lying, drugs, alcohol; those who follow their heroes without any regard for what they do.) **Can you describe some times you have had to stand firm in your faith?** Allow for responses. **Can you think of a time when you had to have courage and be strong at school?** (It might be taking a test or learning something new. Maybe it was facing a person or group of people that was pressuring you to do something you didn't want to do.)

This week, let's work toward the goal of being a hero at school. Look for ways you can be on guard, stand firm in your faith, and be strong and courageous. Let all your actions begin with a loving attitude!

Living the Lesson (5-10 minutes)

End today's session by encouraging your students to set some goals about what kind of legacy they would like to be remembered for. **The list of accomplishments Josiah made in his lifetime are pretty impressive. He had a plan and kept to it! What kind of legacy do you want to leave? What would you like to be remembered for? How would you want others to describe you? You're not too young to begin thinking about those goals and ideas.** Have the students complete the last portion of the activity sheet "Josiah's Royal Legacy." Ask them to write at least three lifetime goals that would allow them to leave the kind of legacy they would want. Examples of nonspecific goals are: (1) Follow God's leading for my life, (2) Always be honest, (3) Care for others.

Close today's session in a time of prayer thanking God for the potential of each child. Ask for God's guidance and direction in each of their lives. Leave the kids with the parting words—Live a legacy this week!

Circles of Influence

Why do you do what you do? Wear what you wear? Do you know who your influences are? Write down some things about yourself and then answer the questions.

THE WAY I TALK

Popular phrases I use:

_____

_____

Where they came from:

_____

_____

PICK ONE OF YOUR ALL-TIME FAVORITE HEROES. WHAT ONE WAY WOULD YOU LIKE MOST TO BE LIKE THAT PERSON?

THE WAY I DRESS

What I wear:

_____

_____

Who set the example:

_____

_____

GAMES I CHOOSE TO PLAY

Name of game:

_____

_____

Hero I like best:

_____

_____

THE SHOES I BUY

Name or type of shoe:

_____

_____

Who endorses or wears that brand:

_____

_____

THE DRINKS I CHOOSE

My favorite drink:

_____

_____

Who else drinks it:

_____

_____

THE FOOD I EAT

My favorite food:

_____

_____

Who else eats it:

_____

_____

 **Josiah's Royal Legacy**

There were 39 years in Josiah's life. Can you mark the time life to indicate how old he was when some important events happened?
Check the Scripture references and write what these events were.
What do you think you might be doing at those ages in your life? Write some ideas about yourself next to that age for Josiah.

_____/_____
Birth   **8**   _____   _____   _____   **Death**
          years
          old

	In my life:	In Josiah's life
8 years old: (see II Chronicles 34:1)	_____ _____	_____ _____
16 years old: (see II Chronicles 34:3)	_____ _____	_____ _____
20 years old: (see II Chronicles 34:3-7)	_____ _____	_____ _____
26 years old: (see II Chronicles 34:8)	_____ _____	_____ _____
39 years old: (see II Chronicles 34:1)	_____ _____	_____ _____

JOSIAH has gone down in History!! He is now famous for . . .
1. II CHRONICLES 34:2 (II Kings 22:2) _____
2. II CHRONICLES 35:18 _____
3. II CHRONICLES 35:25 _____

YOU will go down in History!! What would you like to be famous for?
1. _____
2. _____
3. _____

Lesson 3

Quality You Can Count On!

Aim: That your students will learn how patterning their lives after godly heroes and heroines can make them heroes to others.

Scripture: II Kings 5:1-14

Unit Verse: Join with others in following my example, brothers, and take note of those who live according to the pattern we gave you. Philippians 3:17

Unit Affirmation: I CAN HAVE HEROES TO ADMIRE AND RESPECT!

 **Planning Ahead**

1. Photocopy Activity Sheets (pages 111 and 112)—one for each student. If possible, photocopy the first sheet (the cube) onto cardstock.
2. **OPTIONAL:** Bake two batches of cookies or brownies, one by following the recipe closely, the other omitting the sugar. Have at least one cookie from each batch for each student.
3. Prepare the following supplies for the Unit Verse bulletin board: a picture of a church (preferably your own church) or the word CHURCH written in large letters, the words of Exodus 20:8 written on a large piece of paper.

1 Setting the Stage (5-10 minutes)

WHAT YOU'LL DO

- Attempt to make a cube without the help of instructions or a pattern
- Discuss the difficulty of making something without direction

WHAT YOU'LL NEED

- Rulers, scissors, glue, tape, stapler

2 Introducing the Issue (20 minutes)

WHAT YOU'LL DO

- **OPTIONAL:** Taste the difference between a recipe followed closely and one with an important ingredient left out
- Use an activity sheet to look at godly heroes
- Construct a cube using a pattern
- Add a phrase to the Unit Affirmation poster

WHAT YOU'LL NEED

- **OPTIONAL:** Two batches of cookies
- A sewing pattern or printed assembling directions with a completed picture
- "A Pattern for Success" Activity sheet (page 111)
- Unit Affirmation poster

3 Searching the Scriptures (20 minutes)

WHAT YOU'LL DO

- Discuss how a young servant girl became a hero by saving her master's life
- **OPTIONAL:** Write a diary of the hero's feelings and experiences
- Use an activity sheet to decode our pattern for living as godly heroes.

WHAT YOU'LL NEED

- "Recipes for Success" Activity Sheet (page 112)

4 Living the Lesson (5-10 minutes)

WHAT YOU'LL DO

- Discuss being a hero at school

WHAT YOU'LL NEED

- Unit Verse bulletin board

 *Lesson 3*

Setting the Stage (5-10 minutes)

As your students arrive today, give each one a piece of paper and a pencil. Have scissors, tape, glue, stapler, and ruler available. Their assignment is to construct a cube out of the paper. Do not give them any further instruction or a sample to follow. Students may work alone or in groups of two. When all have arrived, ask for volunteers to share their "finished product." **Have any of you ever constructed a cube before? Did you find it easy or difficult to make? What could have made it easier to construct a sturdy cube?** (A pattern to follow.)

If you've made a cube before, you have some idea of what is involved. If not, you may have been really frustrated! Having a pattern or instructions can really help! They provide the steps necessary to achieve the end result. Today we're going to talk about how patterns and instructions can help us in everyday life. And especially how patterning our lives after godly people (heroes) can produce godliness in us!

Introducing the Issue (20 minutes)

OPTIONAL: Explain to your class that you decided to bring a special treat today, cookies! Tell them that when you first started, you thought you had the recipe memorized and so you did it without looking at the recipe. However, you don't think they taste quite right; what do the kids think? Ask volunteers to help distribute the first samples (the ones without the sugar). Let them eat these cookies and tell you what they think. Then say that you decided to try again, this time following the recipe. Distribute the complete recipe versions.

Both cookies you just ate were the same type (chocolate chip, oatmeal). **How were they different? Which one did you like best? Why? It is essential that you follow the recipe when you are cooking. But what happens when you don't follow the recipe exactly? Does it affect the outcome of the product?** (Yes!) **Some ingredients are more crucial that others, but leaving out even one ingredient changes the entire taste of the recipe.** Explain that the first cookie they ate did not contain any sugar. By tasting the difference between these two cookies, you can see how leaving out just one important ingredient can make a big difference!

Instructions and patterns help to make our lives easier. Can you think of some other things that are much easier to do with a pattern or in-

structions? (Sewing, assembling a toy, building a model, operating a machine for the first time.) **Have any of you ever failed to do something successfully because you didn't take time to follow a pattern or the instructions?** Allow kids to share experiences. Display the directions or sewing pattern. Explain that the picture shows what the finished product should look like. If the pattern pieces and instructions are followed carefully, you will produce the desired outcome. Explain that heroes can be just like this pattern. We can look at the way they have lived their lives, draw on their experience and example, and use them to learn and develop in some of the same ways.

Both the recipe and the pattern or directions provide us with a goal and some specific steps, already tried and tested, to achieve that goal. Can you think of some tools, patterns, or people we can use as patterns to guide our lives? (Possibilities are: Bible, books, teachers, parents, grandparents, friends, pastors, coaches.) **God especially knew that we as humans would need heroes and patterns to help make our lives successful. What patterns or heroes did He provide for us?** (The Bible, Jesus, heroes throughout history, other people in our lives.) **By following these patterns, we can learn how to live the way God has planned for us to live. Let's see what we can learn from some of God's heroes.**

Distribute copies of the activity sheet "A Pattern for Success" (page 111) and Bibles. Divide the class in to six groups and give each group one of the Scripture references to look up. Each group is to record the name of the hero and at least two qualities or characteristics on the chalkboard or a large piece of paper, so all the information can be read by everyone else. Have the kids write the names of all the heroes on the sides of the cube. Discuss how these persons are heroes, and how they have provided us with patterns to guide our lives today.

1. Daniel 1:4, 8; 5:16, 17; 6:10, 26-28 (DANIEL: obedient, brave, bold, disciplined) **What qualities did Daniel need to stand his ground?**
2. Judges 4:4-6, 14 (DEBORAH: good decision maker, brave, good leader, obedient, independent) **How do you think Deborah felt leading the troops?**
3. Exodus 2:3-8; 15:20; Micah 6:4 (MIRIAM: caring, brave, leader, bold, protective) **What characteristics can we learn from her willingness to protect her baby brother?**
4. Luke 5:1-11; Acts 3:1-7 (PETER: bold, leader, unselfish, outspoken, fearless, decisive) **Peter gave up all he had and followed Jesus. What traits would help us follow his example?**
5. Joshua 2:1-15 (RAHAB: courageous, sensible, protective, obedient, deci-

sive) **In spite of her fear, Rahab did what needed to be done.**
6. Joshua 1:1, 5-8; 6:2, 27 (JOSHUA: leader, brave, obedient, faithful) **What qualities did he portray to accomplish God's task?**

Now let the kids cut out and assemble the cube. Compare this cube with the ones they made earlier. Talk about how with the right outline and instructions the job is much easier! Encourage them to keep the cube as a reminder of some of God's best heroes and what their lives teach us about godly living.

For the last few weeks we've been talking about heroes and how they provide an example and a pattern for us. We've also seen how we become like the heroes we choose for our lives. But the most important thing to realize is that as we follow the examples of our heroes, we are setting the same example for others around us. That's why it is so important for us to choose heroes who help us become more and more like the people God intends for us to be. By following their examples, we can become heroes to the people around us!

Display the Unit Affirmation poster. Read the Affirmation and phrases listed so far. Ask the kids to think of a phrase to add this week. It could be, "Heroes give me a pattern for becoming a hero myself." or "Heroes give me an example to follow." **We've looked at some famous Bible heroes that are patterns for us. Once again, let's remember that even kids can be heroes as we look at a young Bible heroine who made a big difference!**

Searching the Scriptures (20 minutes)

Introduce today's lesson by giving some background information on leprosy. Leprosy is an infectious disease caused by a microorganism that attacks the skin. It causes discolored patches, nodules and ulcers. Eventually the nerves laying under the skin are damaged causing loss of sensory perception and partial paralysis. That means people with leprosy lose feeling in their limbs. They cannot feel hot or cold, sharp or dull. In extreme cases a portion of the limb might even fall off.

Today we have medicines and treatment to stop it, but at that time there was no cure. It was not only physically painful, but also emotionally painful. Lepers were not allowed to be around well people. They were usually sent away from family, towns, and villages. It was a lonely, painful, and debilitating disease!

How many of you have ever known someone with leprosy? It is not a common disease in our country today, but in Bible times it was a terrible and dreaded condition! Do you think you could live a very happy or productive life with this disease? Why or why not? Today we're going

to learn about a famous commander of Syria's army who had the disease of leprosy. Ask class members to open their Bibles to II Kings 5. Choose a student to read the first verse. **How is Naaman described?** (Commander of the army of the king of Aram, great man in the sight of his master, high regarded valiant soldier, leper.) **Based on what we've described of the disease, what problems could leprosy cause an army commander?** (Troops wouldn't want to be around him. They might not follow his command. He would be in pain in battle. He might not know if he was injured in battle.)

Ask a student to read verse two. **How do you think it would feel to be captured by enemy soldiers and given to one of the officers' wives as a servant? Who is the prophet she referred to?** (Elisha. It is likely that this young girl had witnessed or heard about some of the miracles God had performed through Elisha, and saw this as a way to help Naaman.)

Ask a student to read I Kings 5:4-6. **Do you think it took a lot of faith on Naaman's part to approach the king? Why or why not?** (On the recommendation of a young captured girl, he was asking to go to a conquered nation for help. The king might not have believed the girl and might have been offended by this request.)

Read I Kings 5:7-12. Explain that the Jordan River was on foreign soil and was known for being dirty. Naaman was upset because he expected to be healed by the magical work of Elisha and did not expect to have to do anything. Elisha insulted him by not talking to him directly. His directions required obedience and faith on Naaman's part. Naaman refers to the Abana and Pharpar rivers (verse 12) because they were in his own country. But God was trying to show Naaman that it was His power that would save him and not the gods and idols of his own nation.

Choose a student to read verse 14 and tell what happened. **Naaman was healed! But the story doesn't end there. Let's read the next verse and see what happened?** Read verse 15. **Naaman declares that there is no God in all the world except in Israel. He did not believe that until he was healed! Because of the young servant who was very much aware of God's power, and her willingness to share her knowledge, God was able to work a miracle! As a result, Naaman was healed both inside and out. He had new skin and a new faith in the one and only true God. How do you think Naaman's friends and troops reacted to his healing?** (Some might have also put their faith in the true God.) **Through the actions of this one captive servant girl, the lives of many people were changed.**

OPTIONAL: If time allows, have your students create a diary from the servant girl's perspective. You might divide the class into pairs and let each pair write

a different entry. Record how she might have felt during the invasion of her country, as she was captured, when she was given to Naaman's wife, and during the healing process. After a few minutes, let kids read their pages to each other.

Distribute copies of the activity sheet "Recipes for Success" (page 112). Let the kids have fun completing the first portion of the sheet by adding the described words to make a silly recipe. **God knew we would need help in living our lives. He gave us some important ingredients that would lead to success in living the life of a hero.** Instruct students to decode the words to discover some of God's ingredients for heroic living. The answers are: Bible, Ten Commandments, prayer, the life of Jesus. Then discuss how each can be an effective tool to help them make life decisions and choose standards to live by.

Living the Lesson (5-10 minutes)

There are many places in our lives where we can be heroes. Direct attention to the Unit Verse bulletin board. Review the verses listed so far and the locations you have talked about. **This week we'll add another place to our board.** (Attach word or picture of "Church" to board.) **That may seem like a strange place to be a hero, but your actions and attitudes in church can be an example to others. You could invite a friend to church with you. Like the servant girl in our Bible lesson, you could be an influence to help others come to see and experience God's power in their lives.**

End today's session with a prayer that God will help each of your students to live as His heroes in every area of their lives—home, school, and church!

A Pattern for Success ✔

Daniel 1:4, 8; 5:16, 17; 6:10, 26-28
HERO'S
NAME:_____
QUALITIES I ADMIRE:

_____
_____
_____

Judges 4:4-6, 14
HERO'S
NAME:_____
QUALITIES I ADMIRE:

_____
_____
_____

Exodus 2:3-8; 15:20; Micah 6:4
HERO'S
NAME:_____
QUALITIES I ADMIRE:

_____
_____
_____

Luke 5:1-11; Acts 3:1-7
HERO'S
NAME:_____
QUALITIES I ADMIRE:

_____
_____
_____

Joshua 2:1-15
HERO'S
NAME:_____
QUALITIES I ADMIRE:

_____
_____
_____

Joshua 1:1, 5-8; 6:2, 27
HERO'S
NAME:_____
QUALITIES I ADMIRE:

_____
_____
_____

RECIPE FOR FUN

NAME OF DISH: _____ _____
                              (adjective)   (food)

Mix 2 cups _____ _____
                              (adjective)   (noun)

and 3 tablespoons of _____ _____
                                      (adjective)   (liquid)

and beat vigorously. Add 4 _____ eggs
                                              (name of an animal)

and pour into a baking dish. Bake at _____ degrees for
                                                          (number)

_____ hours. This recipe serves _____ and should be
(number)   (number)

served for _____. (name of holiday)

Fortunately God gave us some serious ingredients for success. Decode the following words to discover what ingredients we can use to lead a godly life. Unfortunately, there is an unwanted ingredient in the scrambled words AND the letters are not in the correct order However, the solution is worth working for!

RECIPE FOR SUCCESS:

Mix one KEKLKBKIKB _____ with

NKEKKTK SKTKNKKEKMKDKNKAKMKKMKOKC _____.

Add KRKEKKYKAKRKP_____ and EKKHKT KEKFKKIKLK

FKOKK KSKUKSKKKEKJ _____.

Take some every day to become the hero God intends you to be!

Everybody Needs This Hero

Aim: That you students will identify Jesus as the ideal hero and choose to follow Him, patterning their lives after His example.

Scripture: Philippians 2:5-11

Unit Verse: Join with others in following my example, brothers, and take note of those who live according to the pattern we gave you. Philippians 3:17

Unit Affirmation: I CAN HAVE HEROES TO ADMIRE AND RESPECT!

 **Planning Ahead**

1. Photocopy Activity Sheets (pages 119 and 120)—one for each student.
2. Make Puzzle Game pieces as described in INTRODUCING THE ISSUE.
3. Prepare the following materials for the Unit Verse bulletin board: a picture of friends or the word FRIENDS printed in large letters, and the words of Luke 6:31 written on a large piece of paper.

1 Setting the Stage (5-10 minutes)

WHAT YOU'LL DO

- Brainstorm about and draw the perfect hero

WHAT YOU'LL NEED

- "My Hero" Activity Sheet (page 119)

2 Introducing the Issue (20 minutes)

WHAT YOU'LL DO

- Discuss attributes of a Super Hero
- Use the Bible to emphasize Jesus as the ideal hero
- Add the last phrase to the Unit Affirmation poster

WHAT YOU'LL NEED

- Puzzle Game pieces
- Unit Affirmation poster

3 Searching the Scriptures (20 minutes)

WHAT YOU'LL DO

- Examine both the powerful and serving attributes of Jesus
- Present an opportunity for children to accept Jesus as Savior
- Use an activity sheet to learn about our attitudes
- Add the final section to the Unit Verse bulletin board

WHAT YOU'LL NEED

- "Just Like Jesus" Activity Sheet (page 120)
- Unit Verse bulletin board

4 Living the Lesson (5-10 minutes)

WHAT YOU'LL DO

- Participate in a mirror-image activity
- Name ways we can become more like Jesus

WHAT YOU'LL NEED

- **OPTIONAL:** a large mirror

 *Lesson 4*

Setting the Stage (5-10 minutes)

As children arrive today give each one a copy of the activity sheet "My Hero!" (page 119). Their assignment is to draw a picture of the perfect hero on the blank side of the paper. This person may be real or fictional. They may want to design their own "perfect hero."

After drawing their hero, have them complete the questions on the worksheet to focus on specific information about their own hero. As children work, circulate around the room asking questions and giving encouragement. **What qualities are you showing in your hero? Do you have any of those qualities in your own life? Have you ever met your hero in person? Would you like to meet your hero?**

When all have arrived, ask several volunteers to share their ideas. **How many of you chose the same hero? How many created your own idea of a hero?** Have kids explain why they created him or her the way they did. **You've all worked hard to come up with just the right combination of qualities and descriptions. Now let's see if we can identify an authentic, #1 perfect hero!**

Introducing the Issue (20 minutes)

Before class, write each of these six Scripture references in large letters on separate 8 1/2" x 5 1/2" pieces of construction paper. Print each reference on a different color paper. Cut each paper into several pieces, using jigsaw puzzle style cuts. Each student will need one piece of one of the puzzles. Wait to cut one or two of the puzzles until after class begins so you will have the exact number of pieces needed. Psalm 23:1, Psalm 24:8, Psalm 145:13b, Isaiah 9:6, II Samuel 22:3, Luke 24:19.

We all had some different ideas on what makes the perfect hero, but there were some characteristics that came up several times. Let's think back over all the heroes shared and make a list of the qualities we think are most important. Make a list of what the class agrees upon as the most important traits. Some suggestions are: strong, powerful, intelligent, caring, loving, honest, trustworthy, loyal, awesome, leader, fearless, bold. **This is a pretty impressive list of qualifications, isn't it? It may seem as if there is no one in all the world who could live up to all these qualifications, but there is. Who is it?** (Jesus!) **Let's look at some of the things we can learn about Jesus that makes Him the perfect hero.**

Mix up the puzzle pieces for the Puzzle Game and give each student one

piece. They are to locate the students who have the matching color, and put their puzzle together. After looking up the Scripture reference in a Bible, each group is to look for words that describe Jesus and write those words on the chalkboard or large piece of paper.

After each group has found and written their descriptive words, talk about how these qualities are important to each of us when we think about Jesus as our hero.

1. Shepherd: Synonyms—Leader, caretaker, provider. Stress the fact that Jesus protects, provides, and loves us. He is concerned with the details of our lives.

2. Strong and mighty: There are times when we feel weak. It is comforting to know that Jesus will always be our strength!

3. Faithful to promises and loving to all He's made: Emphasize the fact that most of us break promises at one time or another. Jesus NEVER breaks a promise.

4. Wonderful Counselor: How many of you have counselors at school? What is their job? (Offer advice, help make decisions, guide and direct you.) Jesus will do the same for each one of us. Mighty God: Discuss the meaning of the word "Mighty." **Everlasting Father:** He will always be! God is even more than the ideal human father. **Prince of Peace:** Jesus is the source of peace.

5. Rock, Fortress, Deliverer: A place of protection. Jesus wants to be a safe place for each of us.

6. Prophet, Powerful in word and deed: Jesus knows the future and tells us about it accurately. He not only talked in powerful ways, but He backed up His powerful words with powerful action. **Can you think of some of the miracles He performed?**

Display a blank "My Hero!" activity sheet. Ask the class to help complete the sheet together using information they have just gathered about Jesus. **No hero of the past or future can ever compare to Jesus! He is the perfect hero! He is all powerful, all loving, and all knowing! These are some of the reasons each one of us should look to him as our #1 Hero!**

Display the Unit Affirmation poster and ask the class to read it aloud. Think together about a phrase you could add today. Possibilities include "Jesus is the Perfect Hero" or "Jesus is my #1 Hero." Record the phrase on the last line of the poster. **No matter how many other heroes we have in our lives, none of them can come close to having all the characteristics that Jesus has. His greatness is more than any of us could ever understand. But there is more. Now let's take a closer look at a different side of Jesus, the #1 hero!**

✓ Searching the Scriptures (20 minutes)

Almost all of the qualities we just listed show the strong side of Jesus—His strength, power, healing, and protection. But the Bible tells us that even though Jesus was all these things and lived in heaven with God, He was willing to give it all up to come to earth. Listen to this passage describing the attitude of Jesus. Read Philippians 2:5-8 to the class. **How is Jesus described?** (Servant, made in human likeness, humble, obedient.) Help your class recognize that Jesus had lots of reasons to be happy where He was. After all, He is God! He lived in heaven and did not have to live in a world with the limitations of a human body. **But the Bible tells us that He loved us so much He was willing to come to earth as a man. He became a servant, a human who was humble and obedient. He even obeyed God by dying on the cross for our sins. Think of all He gave up for us!**

Which verse in this passage tells us that Jesus is a hero we should pattern our lives after? Refer back to verse five. The beginning of this verse says that our attitude is to be the same as that of Christ Jesus. **That means that no matter what our position in life, we can live as servants for God. We can be humble and obedient to Him.**

Distribute copies of the activity sheet "Just Like Jesus" (page 120). Have the kids read the cartoon captions and draw a line to the word that best describes the scene: serving, humble or obedient.

Brainstorm some specific examples of how they can follow Jesus' example to be a servant, humble and obedient this week. Some examples are: SERVING —Helping around the house, cleaning their rooms, helping a teacher after school. HUMBLE - Choosing to do something they normally wouldn't do. Visiting an elderly neighbor. Putting someone else's feelings ahead of their own. Letting someone else go first. OBEDIENT—Obeying parents and teachers the first time they are asked to do something. Following class or home rules.

> **OPTIONAL:** If time allows, divide into small groups and let the kids act out the scenes on the activity sheet or other suggestions.

Direct attention to the Unit Verse bulletin board. Briefly review the places and verses named so far. Remind them that these are all places they can follow the example of their #1 hero by being a servant, humble and obedient. Ask if anyone has done something this past week to be a hero in one of these places. Then give them an opportunity to guess where they think the last location might be. Place the word or picture of FRIENDS on the board. **How many of**

you spend time with friends? What might make it hard to be a hero with friends? (You may want to go along with plans even if you shouldn't. You may have differences of opinion about things.) **Being a friend and an example to others is not always easy!** Add Luke 6:31 to the board. Explain that this verse instructs us to treat others as we want to be treated. **What are some ways we could use this verse with our friends?** (Let everyone have a chance to be a part. Consider their feelings. Put yourself in their place.) Review the Unit Verse one more time. **Remember, wherever we are, we can allow Jesus to be the pattern for the way we treat others.**

This may be a good time to have prayer with those in your class who may never have had the opportunity to make Jesus their #1 hero. Because of His willingness and actions, God honored Jesus. Read Philippians 2:9-11. This portion of the passage talks about the fact that someday, everyone will know that Jesus Christ is Lord. Ask your students if they have discovered Jesus as Lord for themselves. If they have never done so, give them an opportunity to do so. You might want to provide some written materials that explain to a child how to become a Christian. Briefly review the need to believe that Jesus is the Son of God and pray together.

✓ Living the Lesson (5-10 minutes)

In the last few weeks we've talked a lot about heroes and we've also seen the importance of patterning our lives after godly heroes. Here's a way to clearly emphasize what it means to pattern our lives after someone else. Divide the class into pairs. Have each pair face each other. The goal of this exercise is to move together as if looking into a mirror. Demonstrate by doing some mime patterns against a large mirror. Instruct the pairs to choose which person will be the pattern to follow. That child should then begin to slowly move hands or legs. They can make facial expressions, shake their head or stand on tiptoe. The other child is to imitate the leader of the pair exactly.

Give the kids a few minutes to work out a routine. Ask for volunteers to show their movements to the class.

Each of you just had an opportunity to follow someone else's every move and expression. Was it easy or difficult? Allow for responses. **Did it grow easier as you worked together?** (You begin to know what to expect after practice.) **In order to imitate someone or pattern our lives after them, we must know a lot about them. The more we study their movements the easier it is to anticipate how they will act.**

Jesus is our #1 hero, and the best pattern we have for our lives. If we are going to have the same attitudes as Jesus then we need to study His attitudes and actions. What are some ways we can learn more about Jesus? (Read and study the Bible, go to church, pray, spend time with other people who know Him well, read books, listen to the pastor in church, memorize Scripture.) Make a list of suggestions on the board. Encourage each child to think about this mirror activity during the week. As they go through the week, encourage them to picture themselves mirroring Jesus' actions and attitudes in all they do. Ask each child to pick a specific way they will try to be more like Jesus this week.

My Hero! ✓

On the reverse side of this sheet, draw a picture of your perfect hero or heroine. Then fill in the information about him or her below:

| NAME: |
| HOMETOWN: |
| OCCUPATION: |
| WORKING HOURS: |
| SPECIAL SKILLS: |
| FAVORITE PASTIME: |
| SPECIAL NICKNAMES OR ALIAS: |
| THINGS HE SAYS ABOUT HIMSELF OR HERSELF: |
| WEAKNESSES OR VULNERABILITIES: |
| THINGS OTHERS SAY ABOUT HIM OR HER: |
| WORDS THAT DESCRIBE MY HERO: |

 **Just Like Jesus**

Just Like Jesus

Circle the word that best describes the actions in each cartoon strip. Then write one way you can imitate that action this week.

120

Service Projects for Heroes

Your class can have a good time learning about heroes. Use some of the following activities to experience following a hero and being a hero!

✔ 1. Host a hero! Invite a hero to make a guest appearance during class time. Choose a person from your congregation and interview them during class time. Some likely candidates might include: veterans of war, police officers, paramedics, nurses, or sports figures.

✔ 2. Have a hero party! Use this unit as an excuse for a costume party. Invite your kids to dress up as their favorite hero and come equipped with at least three facts about that person. After guests arrive, spend some time introducing your heroes and sharing their facts. Serve hero sandwiches to eat!

✔ 3. Be a hero! Adopt a younger class at your church for three months. Assign one child from your class to be a "big buddy" for a child in the younger class. Design a craft activity so your class can make a small gift for each student in the younger class. Have a party including both classes. Have the "big buddies" serve as hosts for the younger children. Encourage kids from your class to greet their "buddies" when they see them around the church grounds. Provide an opportunity for letters to be written to the "buddies."

✔ 4. Act like a hero! Choose some families in your church who need some work done around their homes. Arrange for a time when your class can do yard work or housework for them. Make a party of it. Take along cookies and lemonade and enjoy a day of fun and hard work.